N. E. W. Chapman M. A. Can

Former Chief Examiner in O-level
Modern Mathematics, London
School Examinations Council
Awarder in O-level Mathematics,
Oxford and Cambridge Board
and
Sometime Head of Mathematics,
Cheshunt Grammar School

Interface Mathematics

A mainstream course for secondary schools

PUPIL'S BOOK 1

HART-DAVIS EDUCATIONAL

First published 1982 by

Hart-Davis Educational Limited
Frogmore, St Albans, Hertfordshire
AL2 2NF

Copyright © N. E. W. Chapman
All rights reserved. No part of this publication may be reproduced, stored in a retrieval system, or transmitted in any form or by any means, electronic, mechanical, photocopying, recording or otherwise, without the prior permission of the publishers.

ISBN 0 247 13174 1

Typeset and printed by Unwin Brothers Ltd, The Gresham Press, Old Woking, Surrey

Cover and book design by Andrew Haig
Chapter heading illustration by Alma R. Duncan
Mathematical illustrations by Sean MacGarry

Granada ®
Granada Publishing ®

Contents

Introduction

Chapter

1	Sets and subsets	8
2	Relations, mappings and functions	16
3	Reflection	23
4	Composite mappings and functions	30
5	Rotation	36
6	Large and small numbers	46
7	Matrices	54
8	Translation and vectors	62
9	Inequalities	77
10	Enlargement and similarity	86
11	Statistics	105
12	More sets	117
13	Factors and quadratic equations	129
14	Probability	139
15	Trigonometry – the tangent	150
	Revision exercises on preliminary work	163
	Revision exercises on chapters 1 to 5	171
	Revision exercises on chapters 6 to 10	178

Preliminary work

It is assumed that students embarking on this mainstream course will be familiar with the topics named in the following list. The books therefore do not cover these topics, but there are some revision examples on them at the end of Book 1.

Basic arithmetic, including calculations with metric weights and measures.

Prime numbers, factors, multiples, indices (positive integral indices only).

Fractions and decimals, including conversion from one to the other.

Ratio, proportion, proportional parts, percentage, simple interest.

Approximation, degree of accuracy, decimal places, significant figures.

Area of a rectangle, triangle, trapezium, and figures that can be built up from these.

Volume of a rectangular parallelepiped (cuboid), prism, pyramid, and figures that can be built up from these.

Mensuration of the circle, cylinder, cone, sphere. Length of an arc and area of a sector of a circle.

Positive and negative numbers.

Construction and use of formulae.

Manipulation of simple algebraic expressions, removing brackets, collecting terms, multiplication of simple expressions, fractions with numerical denominators.

Solution of linear (simple) equations with one or two unknowns.

Meaning of square root, use of square root tables, rational and irrational numbers. Cartesian coordinates, equations of straight lines when these are very simple, e.g. $x=y$, $y=3$.

Simple statistical graphs including 'pie-charts'.

Measurement and classification of angles. Angle properties of parallel lines.

Properties and classification of triangles and quadrilaterals. Angles of polygons.

Symmetry of plane figures. Congruence.

Pythagoras' Theorem.

The simpler constructions, e.g. the perpendicular bisector of a straight line.

Bearings.

Questions from the O-level papers of various examining boards are indicated as follows:

AEB	Associated Examining Board for the General Certificate of Education
CB, CC, CD	University of Cambridge Local Examinations Syndicate, Syllabus B, C or D
LB, LC, LD	University of London University Entrance and School Examinations Council, Syllabus B, C or D
OC	Oxford and Cambridge Schools Examination Board
16+	East Anglian and Cambridge Joint Examinations at 16+

The author and publishers would like to thank the boards for their permission to reproduce these questions.

I should like to thank my colleague Mrs E. Brown for her work in checking the manuscript and the answers to the examples. I am also grateful to many pupils at various schools, especially Berkhamsted School for Girls, for cheerfully acting as 'guinea pigs'. On these pupils were tried out many of the examples and all the projects, experiments, practical work and games described in the whole of this series of books.

Chapter 1

Sets and subsets

A *set* can be any collection of things, called its *members*: in the picture, the individual stamps are the members of the set formed by the collection. Very often, however, the members are not 'things' in the usual sense – they may be people, or numbers, or indeed anything that can form a collection.

A set can be named in *list form*, as {red, white, blue}, or in *title form*, as {colours of the British flag}. Either way, the name is put between curved brackets, called *braces*.

For convenience, sets are often named by letters of the alphabet: we could write $C=${red, white, blue}. The letter is *not* put between braces.

The order in which the members of the set are named does not matter, so that $C=${blue, white, red}$=${white, red, blue}.

CHAPTER 1 — SETS AND SUBSETS

When a set is named in list form, no member is mentioned more than once, so that {letters of the word NOON}={N, O}.

The symbol ∈ means 'is a member of', so red ∈ C

The symbol ∉ means 'is not a member of', so green ∉ C.

Example 1 Write $N=\{1, 2, 3, 4\}$ in title form and state which of the following are true:
$2 \in N$, $2 \notin N$, $5 \in N$, $5 \notin N$.

Answer

$N=$ {the four smallest whole numbers}, or {whole numbers less than 5} (note, not just 'whole numbers').
It is true that $2 \in N$ and that $5 \notin N$, but not true that $2 \notin N$ or that $5 \in N$.

Exercise 1.1

In this exercise, 'numbers' means 'whole numbers'.

1 Name each of the following sets in list form.

  a {the days of the week}
  b {the continents of the world}
  c {capitals of countries of the United Kingdom}
  d {months whose names contain the letter R}
  e {English words that can be formed from the letters O, P, S, T, using each letter just once}
  f {seasons of the year}
  g {numbers that are more than 3 but less than 10}
  h {even numbers that are less than 13}
  i {numbers that can be obtained by multiplying by 3 a number less than 10}
  j {numbers that are the squares of numbers less than 7}
  k {numbers with 3 digits whose total is 3}
  l {letters of the word MATHEMATICS}
  m {factors of 24, including 1 and 24}
  n {prime factors of 24}

2 Name each of the following sets in title form.

  a {north, east, west, south}
  b {Atlantic, Pacific, Arctic, Antarctic, Indian}
  c {January, June, July}
  d {April, June, September, November}
  e {Mercury, Venus}
  f {A, E, I, O, U}
  g {equilateral, isosceles, scalene}

h {16, 17, 18, 19, 20}
   i {1, 3, 5, 7, 9, 11, 13}
   j {16, 25, 34, 43, 52, 61, 70}
   k {$\frac{1}{4}$, $\frac{1}{2}$, $\frac{3}{4}$}

3 In this question, the sets mentioned in question 1 are given the names A, B, C etc., so that A = {the days of the week} and so on. Say, or write, whether each of the following statements is true or false.

   a Tuesday $\in A$ **e** OPTS $\notin E$ **i** 27 $\notin I$ **m** 8 $\notin M$
   b Asia $\notin B$ **f** June $\notin F$ **j** 81 $\in J$ **n** 8 $\in N$
   c London $\in C$ **g** 3 $\in G$ **k** 21 $\notin K$
   d June $\in D$ **h** 11 $\notin H$ **l** S $\notin L$

4 Make ten more statements like those in question 3, about the sets A to N. In five of your statements use the symbol $\in$, and in the other five use the symbol $\notin$.

5 Make up four sets, naming them either in title or in list form. Name each set also with a letter, and about each set make four statements like those in question 3.

6 In each part of this question, write down statements that two of the given sets are equal, and that the third is not equal to either of them, e.g. $L = M$, $L \neq N$, $M \neq N$.

   a O = {letters of CAT}, P = {letters of PAT}, Q = {letters of ACT}
   b R = {letters of DEED}, S = {letters of RED}, T = {letters of REDDER}
   c U = {even numbers}, V = {numbers, all of whose digits are even}, W = {numbers whose last digits are even}
   d X = {6, 7, 8, 9}, Y = {single-digit numbers larger than 5}, Z = {9, 8, 7, 6, 5}
   e E = {colours of the British flag}, F = {colours of the French flag}, G = {colours of the Swiss flag}
   f H = {prime factors of 20}, I = {prime factors of 30}, J = {prime factors of 40}
   g K = {multiples of 5}, L = {numbers with 5 as last digit}, M = {odd numbers which are multiples of 5}

7 Make up five examples of pairs of sets which are equal but can be described in different ways (not simply by naming the same set in title form and in list form).

8 Make up five examples of pairs of sets which are unequal, but which on casual inspection might appear to be equal.

Subsets

A set is said to be a *subset* of another set if all the members of the first set are also members of the second set: the stamp-collector's French stamps are a subset of his foreign stamps. Again, {1, 2} is a subset of {1, 2, 3, 4} and {multiples of 4} is a subset of {even numbers}.

The symbol $\subset$ means 'is a subset of', so {B, C} $\subset$ {A, B, C, D}.
The symbol $\not\subset$ means 'is not a subset of', so {D, E} $\not\subset$ {A, B, C, D}.
The symbol $\supset$ means 'contains as a subset', so {A, B, C, D} $\supset$ {B, C}.
The symbol $\not\supset$ means 'does not contain as a subset', so {A, B, C, D} $\not\supset$ {D, E}.

Example 2 Make statements using the above symbols, concerning the sets E={even numbers}, F={multiples of 4}, S={multiples of 6}.

Answer
$F \subset E$, $E \supset F$, $S \subset E$, $E \supset S$, $F \not\subset S$, $S \not\supset F$.

Example 3 If F and S have the same meanings as in Example 2, find a subset of F which is also a subset of S.

Answer
A possible subset is {12, 24, 36}; but {multiples of 12} or any subset of {multiples of 12} is a correct answer.

The universal set

Sometimes it is convenient to define a *universal set* which contains as its members everything we are discussing for the time being. For example, if we are going to talk about children in Form IVA, we can let {children in Form IVA} be the universal set and then we can write {children with blue eyes} instead of having to write {children in IVA with blue eyes}. The universal set is usually denoted by the symbol $\mathscr{E}$.

Example 4 If $\mathscr{E}$={numbers between 10 and 30} give the following sets in list form: F={multiples of 4}, S={perfect squares}, P={prime numbers}.

Answer
F={12, 16, 20, 24, 28}, S={16, 25}, P={11, 13, 17, 19, 23, 29}.

The empty set

The set which contains no members at all is called the empty set and is denoted by the symbol $\emptyset$ or by {} (empty braces).

Example 5 If $\mathscr{E}=\{$numbers between 10 and 15$\}$ give the following sets in list form or state if they are empty sets: $F=\{$multiples of 4$\}$, $S=\{$perfect squares$\}$, $E=\{$multiples of 8$\}$.

Answer
$F=\{12\}$, $S=\emptyset$, $E=\emptyset$.

Exercise 1.2

1 Name, either in list or in title form, three different subsets of each of the following sets. Name each subset by a letter, and make statements like $A \subset C$.

   a $C=\{$capitals of countries$\}$
   b $M=\{$letters of MATHEMATICS$\}$
   c $T=\{$people who live in your town or village$\}$
   d $B=\{$books you have read$\}$
   e $E=\{$even numbers with two digits$\}$
   f $S=\{$perfect squares with three digits$\}$
   g $F=\{5, 10, 15, 20, 25, 30\}$
   h $P=\{2, 3, 5, 7, 11, 13, 17\}$

2 For each of the following pairs of sets, if it is correct to write $\subset$ or $\supset$ between the two sets of the pair, write the correct symbol. If not, write $\not\subset$ and $\not\supset$ between them.

   a $\{$cats$\}$ $\{$animals$\}$
   b $\{$cats$\}$ $\{$black animals$\}$
   c $\{$cats$\}$ $\{$black cats$\}$
   d $\{2, 3, 4\}$ $\{$numbers less than 4$\}$
   e $\{2, 3, 4\}$ $\{$numbers less than 5$\}$
   f $\{2, 3, 4\}$ $\{2\}$
   g $\{$letters of PLEASE$\}$ $\{$letters of PLASTER$\}$
   h $\{$letters of PLEASE$\}$ $\{$letters of SLEEP$\}$
   i $\{$letters of PLEASE$\}$ $\{$letters of STEAL$\}$
   j $\{$multiples of 4$\}$ $\{$multiples of 8$\}$
   k $\{$multiples of 4$\}$ $\{$multiples of 6$\}$

3 For each of the sets in Question 1, suggest a suitable universal set, and find another subset of this universal set.

4 If $\mathscr{E}=\{$numbers less than 20$\}$ give the following sets in list form: $T=\{$multiples of 3$\}$, $S=\{$perfect squares$\}$, $F=\{$factors of 60$\}$.

5 If $\mathscr{E}=\{$proper fractions in their lowest terms$\}$ give the following sets in list form: $D=\{$fractions with denominator 6$\}$, $N=\{$fractions with numerator 6 and value more than $\frac{1}{2}\}$.

CHAPTER 1 — SETS AND SUBSETS

6 If $\mathscr{E}$={numbers between 50 and 60}, give the following sets in list form, or state if they are empty sets: S={multiples of 7}, Q={perfect squares}, P={prime numbers}.

7 For each of the following sets, state whether it is empty. Write, for example, $A = \emptyset$ or $A \neq \emptyset$ as the case may be.

a A={English words beginning with X}
b B={letters in the word CAT and also in the word LION}
c C={letters in the word CAT but not in the word LEOPARD}
d D={numbers divisible by 9 and also by 8}
e E={even numbers with last digit 3}
f F={multiples of 7 with last digit 2}
g G={numbers divisible by 4 but not by 8}
h H={numbers divisible by 8 but not by 4}

8 For each of the following pairs of sets, name the most numerous subset of the first which is also a subset of the second:

a {letters of HOUSE}, {letters of SCHOOL}
b {months in the first half of the year}, {months whose names contain the letter E}
c {colours of the French flag}, {colours of the Italian flag}
d {1, 2, 3, 4}, {2, 4, 6, 8}
In parts **e**, **f** and **g**, $\mathscr{E}$={numbers less than 21}
e {even numbers}, {multiples of 4}
f {even numbers}, {multiples of 5}
g {even numbers}, {prime numbers}

9 For each of the pairs of sets in question 8, name the least numerous set of which both are subsets.

Venn diagrams

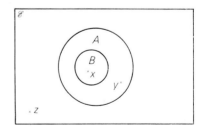

Figure 1.1

The relations between sets and their subsets can be illustrated by means of diagrams, known as **Venn diagrams**, like that shown here. The universal set is usually represented by a rectangle and other sets by other shapes, usually rough circles, inside the rectangle. In the diagram above, the circle for B is inside that for A, showing that B is a subset of A. Individual members, sometimes called **elements**, may be represented by dots or small crosses: in the diagram above we see that x is a member of B, and therefore of A, and that y is a member of A but not of B, while z is a member of neither A nor B.

Example 6 Draw a Venn diagram to illustrate $\mathscr{E}$={numbers less than 25}, E={multiples of 8}, F={multiples of 4}, P={prime numbers}.

Answer
Draw a rectangle for $\mathscr{E}$, and a circle inside it for F. As $E \subset F$, draw the circle for E inside that for F. As P contains no members of F, draw the circle for P outside that for F.

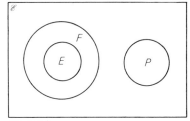

Figure 1.2

Exercise 1.3

1 The Venn diagram (Figure 1.3) represents a universal set $\mathscr{E}$ with subsets P and Q: the small crosses represent elements t and u. State which of the following are true:

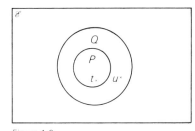

Figure 1.3

a $P \subset Q$ **e** $t \in Q$
b $Q \subset P$ **f** $u \in P$
c $t \in P$ **g** $P \in \mathscr{E}$
d $u \in Q$ **h** $Q \subset \mathscr{E}$

2 Make as many true statements as you can, like those in Question 1, and using only the symbols $\subset$ and $\in$, about the elements a, b and c and the sets X, Y and Z represented in this Venn diagram (Figure 1.4).

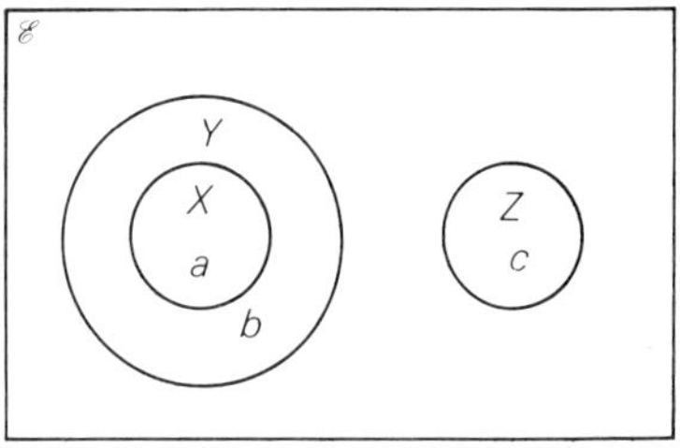

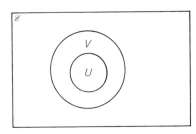

Figure 1.4

3 Copy this diagram (Figure 1.5) and mark a small cross to indicate an element x such that $x \in V$. Must it be true that $x \in U$?
Mark, if possible, a small cross to indicate y so that $y \in U$ but $y \notin V$.
Mark, if possible, a small cross to indicate z so that $z \in V$ but $z \notin U$.
Mark, if possible, a small cross to indicate t so that $t \notin U$ and $t \notin V$.

Figure 1.5

4 Draw a Venn diagram to illustrate $\mathscr{E}$={letters of the alphabet}, X={letters of ESSENTIAL}, Y={letters of SET}. Mark in the positions of the letters S, A, B, T, M.

5 Draw a Venn diagram to illustrate $\mathscr{E}$={towns}, E={towns in England}, S={towns in Scotland}, Y={towns in Yorkshire}. Mark with single letters the positions on the diagram of points representing London, Paris, York, Edinburgh and any other four towns of your own choosing.

6 Draw a Venn diagram to illustrate $\mathscr{E}$={numbers}, E={even numbers}, F={numbers with last digit 4}, N={numbers with last digit 9}. On the diagram mark points to represent 12, 24, 39, 45 and any other four numbers of your own choosing. (Beside each point write the number it represents.)

7 In a certain mixed school some girls, but no boys, play lacrosse; some boys, but no girls, play football. Draw a Venn diagram to illustrate this, drawing circles for G={girls} (What part represents {boys}?), L={lacrosse players} and F={footballers}. Mark and label points to represent

a Alice, a lacrosse-player   **c** Claire, who does not play lacrosse
b Bill, a footballer   **d** Donald, a non-footballer

8 In the sixth form of this school it is ruled that:

a You can take A-level mathematics only if you have passed O-level mathematics
b You can take A-level physics only if you have passed O-level mathematics
c You can take A-level physics only if you are taking A-level mathematics

Draw a Venn diagram to represent the various sets concerned, and find which of the three rules is unnecessary.

9 All towns with cathedrals are cities. Draw a Venn diagram to show $\mathscr{E}$={towns}, C={cities}, X={towns with cathedrals}. Find which of these arguments are sound:

a Lichfield has a cathedral so it is a city
b Cambridge is a city so it has a cathedral
c Ipswich has no cathedral so it is not a city
d Watford is not a city so it has no cathedral

10 All rodents are mammals and all mammals are warm-blooded. Illustrate this with a Venn diagram and find which of the following arguments are sound:

a Birds are warm-blooded so they must be mammals
b Cats are mammals so they must be warm-blooded
c Rats are rodents so they must be warm-blooded
d Frogs are cold-blooded so they cannot be rodents
e Rabbits are mammals so they must be rodents

Chapter 2

Relations, mappings and functions

Relations If we can find any kind of matching between one or more members of one set (called the *domain* set) and one or more members of another set (called the *range* set), we can say that there is a *relation* between the sets. For example, in the picture there is a relation between the domain set {Jane Fox, T. Ash, R. Singh} and the range set {AIF 171 N, HLV 10 G, RVH 473 P}: it is the relation 'owns' and can be illustrated by means of a diagram.

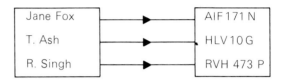

This is a *one-to-one* relation: one owner to one car.

CHAPTER 2 — RELATIONS, MAPPINGS AND FUNCTIONS

If, however, one or more of the cars is jointly owned by two or more people, the relation is *many-to-one*. In this context, 'many' simply means 'more than one', so if HLV 10 G is jointly owned by Mr and Mrs T. Ash, the relation 'owns' between the set of owners and the set of cars is many-to-one, and is illustrated thus:

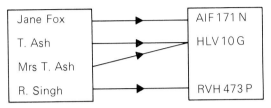

If, on the other hand, none of the cars is jointly owned but one or more of the owners owns more than one car (for example, if R. Singh owns YAI 6 V as well as RVH 473 P), the relation is *one-to-many*. If one or more of the cars is jointly owned *and* one or more of the owners owns more than one car, the relation is *many-to-many*.

Mappings With every relation there is a *mapping* associated. In describing a mapping we describe the member of the range set corresponding to a typical member of the domain set, usually denoted by the letter x. With the relation 'owns', as described above, is associated the mapping '$x \to$ car owned by x', read as 'x maps onto car owned by x'.

Like relations, mappings may be one-to-one, many-to-one, one-to-many, or many-to-many.

A mapping may be denoted by a single letter: if we wish to use the letter c to denote the above mapping, we may write 'c:$x \to$ car owned by x'. The symbol : is read 'is such that', as in other contexts.

Functions A one-to-one or a many-to-one mapping is called a *function*.

Sometimes the domain and range are the same set: in such a case the relation or mapping diagram may be drawn in either of the ways shown below, illustrating the relation 'is opposite to' with the set {north, south, east, west}.

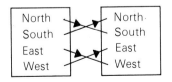 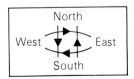

Images The symbol f(x) denotes the member of the range set onto which x maps, using the mapping f; this member is sometimes called the *image* of x. In the example with the cars and their owners, c(Jane Fox) = AIF 171 N, and AIF 171 N is the image of Jane Fox under the mapping c. (The preposition 'under' is, rather strangely, the one normally used in this context.)

Example 1 Draw a diagram to illustrate the relation 'begins with' between the domain set {BAD, BED, CAB, CAD, DAB} and the range set {B, C, D}. What kind of relation is this? Give the associated mapping. Give also the image of BAD under this mapping. If with the same domain set the relation is 'contains', what kind of relation is this, and what must the range set be?

Answer

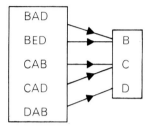

This is a many-to-one relation. The associated mapping is $x \rightarrow$ first letter of x. The image of BAD is B. The relation 'contains' is a many-to-many relation, and the range set is then {A, B, C, D, E}.

Exercise 2.1

1 With domain set {COW, HOW, COT, HOT, TOW} and a suitable range set, draw a relation diagram for the relation 'begins with'. What kind of relation is this?

2 With the same domain set as for Question 1, and with a suitable range set, draw a diagram for the relation 'contains'. What kind of relation is this?

3 In each of Questions 1 and 2, if the domain and range sets were to be interchanged, suggest a suitable name for the resulting relation, and state what kind of relation it is.

4 With domain set {Paris, Madrid, Rome, Brussels} and with a suitable range set, draw a relation diagram for 'is the capital of'. What kind of relation is this?

5 If Lyon, Barcelona, Naples and Antwerp are added to the domain set in Question 4, and the relation changed to 'is in', what kind of relation is this?

6 With domain set {integers between 1 and 12 inclusive} and range set {I, V, X} draw a diagram for the relation 'uses when written as a Roman number'. What kind of relation is this?

CHAPTER 2 — RELATIONS, MAPPINGS AND FUNCTIONS 19

7 Alf, Betty, Charlie, Dorothy and Ed are sitting round a table, not in that order. The partly completed diagram illustrates the relation 'is sitting on the left of'.

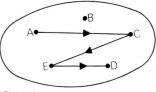

Figure 2.1

a Complete the diagram.
b Draw a sketch to show the order in which the five people are sitting.
c Draw a diagram to show the relation 'is sitting on the right of'. What kind of relation is this?
d Draw a diagram to show the relation 'is sitting next to'. What kind of relation is this?
e Re-draw the diagrams, using separate ovals for domain and range sets.

8 Write in the form '$x \to \ldots$' all the mappings associated with the relations in Questions 1 to 7. State which of these mappings are functions.

9 How may the cast list for a dramatic production be regarded as a relation or a mapping diagram? What could be taken as the domain and what as the range set? What kind of relation or mapping is usually illustrated? Suggest how, on some occasions, the relation or mapping might be of some other kind.

10 Part of the situation at the opening of Shakespeare's *A Midsummer Night's Dream* might be illustrated by the following mapping diagram.

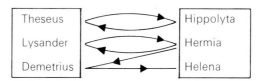

What mapping is illustrated? What kind of mapping is it? Draw further diagrams (adding other characters if necessary) to illustrate the situation

a at the end of Act III,   **b** at the end of the play.

What feature of **b** ensures a happy ending?

11

For the above family tree, draw diagrams to illustrate the following relations.

a 'is married to'   **c** 'is the child of'   **e** 'is the sister of'
b 'is the father of' **d** 'is the parent of'   **f** 'is the cousin of'

For each relation give the associated mapping, and state what kind of mapping it is.

Numerical applications

If the domain and range sets consist of numbers, these are represented by points marked along straight lines: the two sets are always shown on separate lines. Some mappings cannot be applied to certain numbers, which therefore have to be excluded from their domain sets.

Example 2 Draw a mapping diagram for the domain set {1, 2, 3, 4, 5} and the mapping $x \to \frac{12}{x-1}$, omitting that member of the domain set which has to be excluded.

Answer
1 has to be excluded from the domain set, because if $x=1$, $x-1=0$ and it is impossible to divide 12 (or any other number) by 0.

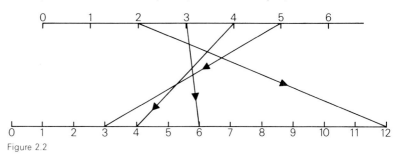

Figure 2.2

Exercise 2.2

1 Draw mapping diagrams for the domain set $\{-2, -1, 0, 1, 2\}$ and each of the following mappings:

    a $x \to 2x$,   **b** $x \to y+3$ **c** $x \to 3-x$ **d** $x \to x^2$

Which of these is not a one-to-one mapping?

2 Name the mapping illustrated by each of the diagrams in Figure 2.3.

3 Give the range set of each of the following mappings, if the domain set is {0, 5, 10, 15}.

    a $x \to x/5$ **b** $x \to 30/(x+5)$ **c** $x \to 5-x$ **d** $x \to \sqrt{10x}$

4 Give the range set of each of the following mappings, if the domain set is {2, 3, 4, 6}.

    a $x \to x/12$ **b** $x \to 12/x$ **c** $x \to 12/(x-5)$ **d** $x \to 12/(5-x)$

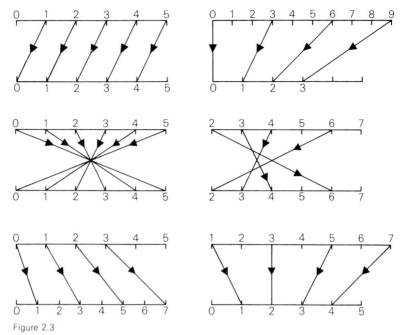

Figure 2.3

5 Draw a mapping diagram for the mapping x→(remainder when x is divided by 3) for the domain set {3, 4, 5, 6, 7, 8}. What kind of mapping is this?

6 If f:x→1/(x−2), give the values of f(0), f(1), f(−1) and f(3). What value of x cannot be mapped by f?

7 Write down the images of 2, 3, 6, 11 and 18 under the mapping x→√(x−2).

8 If g:x→1/x², choose a domain set of four numbers and give the corresponding range set. What value of x must be excluded from the domain set?

9 For each of the following mappings, state which (if any) of the set {1, 2, 3, 4} must be excluded from the domain
  a x→3−x
  b x→1/(3−x)
  c x→√(x−2)
  d x→number which gives x as remainder when divided by 4
  e x→number of which x+1 is a prime factor

10 If f:x→x(x−2), find f(−1), f(0), f(1), f(2) and f(3). What kind of mapping is f?

11 If g:x→2x+5, find the numbers whose images under g are
  a 9   **b** 5   **c** 0   **d** −5

12 If $h: x \to x(x+3)$, find two values of x

    a for which $h(x) = 0$ **b** for which $h(x) = 4$ **c** for which $h(x) = 10$

13 Give the range set of each of the following mappings. State what kind of mapping each is, and whether it is a function.

    a Domain set all numbers including fractions; $x \to$ least integer which is larger than or equal to x.
    b Domain set all numbers, positive and negative; $x \to x^2$.
    c Domain set all integers; $x \to$ a number between x and $x+1$.
    d Domain set all prime numbers; $x \to$ a number which has x as a factor.
    e Domain set all numbers; $x \to \frac{1}{4}x$.
    f Domain set all integers; $x \to$ remainder when x is divided by 4.
    g Domain set $\{1, 2, 3\}$; $x \to$ number which gives x as remainder when divided by 4.

14 Write down expressions for the images under $x \to x+2$ of

    a p **b** $p-2$ **c** p^2 **d** $(p-2)^2$ **e** p^2-2

15 Find expressions for the images under $x \to 5-x$ of

    a y **b** $y+5$ **c** $y-5$ **d** $5-y$

16 If $f(x) = \frac{1}{x}$, find expressions for

    a $f(y)$ **b** $f(\frac{1}{y})$ **c** $f(\frac{2}{3y})$ **d** $f\left(\frac{y+1}{y}\right)$

Chapter 3
Reflection

Reflection can be regarded as a kind of mapping, if the figure which is to be reflected (for example the lady's face in the picture) is regarded as a set of points, forming the domain set. The image of a point A is the point A' such that AA' is bisected perpendicularly by the line of the mirror. (Note that in this context the mathematical use of the word 'image' is the same as its ordinary everyday use.) The range set of image points forms the image figure.

Figure 3.1

Reflection is one kind of *transformation*: other transformations will be described in later chapters.

Drawing the image Two methods are described for drawing the image of a given figure under reflection in a given line L.

Method 1 Fold the paper with L as the fold-line, and the figure on top. Go over the figure with a hard pencil or ball-point, pressing hard so that the figure comes through onto the lower fold of the paper.

Open out the paper.

Go over the pressed-through lines on the *under* side of the paper with a pencil or pen.

Method 2 Mark any point (call it P) on the line L. Lay a piece of tracing paper over the figure and the line L. Trace over the figure, the line L and the point P onto the tracing-paper, using a soft pencil.

Turn the tracing-paper over, and fit the tracing of L over L itself, and the tracing of P over P itself.

Go over the back of the tracing-paper, drawing the figure with a hard pencil or ball-point, pressing hard so that the figure comes through onto the paper. Remove the tracing-paper and go over the image figure again with a pencil or pen.

Exercise 3.1 Images under reflection

1 Copy or trace these figures, and draw their images under reflection in the *thick* vertical or horizontal lines (Figure 3.2).

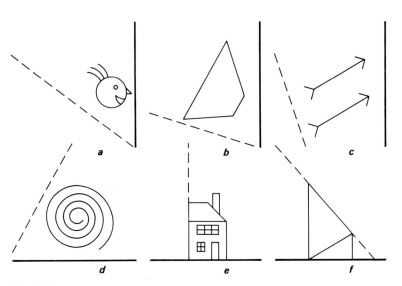

Figure 3.2

2 Repeat Question 1, but this time draw the images under reflection in the broken lines.

3 Draw the letters of the alphabet, or as many of them as your teacher tells you. Use large plain capitals. Draw freehand the image of each letter **a** under reflection in a vertical line to the right of the letter, **b** under reflection in a horizontal line below the letter. Which letters are unchanged (except in position) by the reflection in **a**? Which by the reflection in **b**? Which by both? What can be said about these set of letters?

4 Give the images of the following points under reflection in the x-axis: (1, 3), (−4, 5), (−1, 2), (6, 0), (0, −1), (5, −6), (−2, 7), (4, 3).

5 Give the images of the same points under reflection in the y-axis.

6 Give the images of the same points under reflection in the line $x=y$.

7 Give expressions for the images of the point (p, q) under reflection

   a in the x-axis   **b** in the y-axis   **c** in the line $x=y$.

8 Copy or trace these figures, and draw their images under reflection in the thick lines (Figure 3.3).

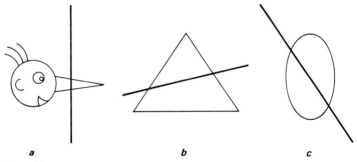

   a   *b*   *c*
Figure 3.3

9 Plot the points (5, −3), (4, 6) and (−2, 4) and join them to form a triangle. Draw the images of this triangle under reflection

   a in the x-axis   **b** in the y-axis

10 Plot the points (3, 1), (3, −1), (−3, 1) and (−3, −1) and join them to form a rectangle. Draw the images of this rectangle under reflection

   a in the line $x=y$ **b** in the line $x+y=0$

11 Draw a straight line l, and mark a point P about 5 cm from it. Draw a circle with centre P, and with radius so large that the circle cuts l at two

points: mark them A and B. With centres A and B, and with the same radius as that used for the circle, draw arcs cutting at Q, on the other side of l from P. Explain why Q is the image of P under reflection in l.

12 Draw a triangle ABC and a straight line l, not passing through A, B or C. Use the result of question 11 to draw the images A', B' and C' of A, B and C under reflection in l, without using tracing paper. Complete the triangle A'B'C'.

13 Figure 3.4 shows the field set by a certain bowler to a right-handed batsman. When a left-handed batsman comes in, the field has to change to its image under reflection in the line joining the wickets. Copy the diagram and draw (in colour) the field positions for the left-handed batsman. Draw arrows to show how some fielders might change positions so as to save time (for example, mid-off might walk a little way and become mid-on).

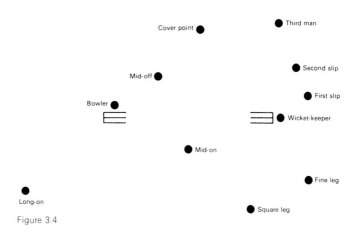

Figure 3.4

Exercise 3.2 Finding the mirror line

1 Make an 'ink devil' by putting a drop or two of ink on a piece of paper, folding the paper while the ink is still wet, opening out and blotting. This gives a figure and its image under reflection in the fold line. Mark a point A and is image A'. Join A'. What is the relation between AA' and the fold line?

2 Mark any two points P and P' on your paper and, using the result of Question 1, draw the mirror line of the reflection which maps P onto P'.

3 Using the 'ink devil' you made for question 1, mark a second point B and its image B'. Join AB' and A'B. Where do these lines cross? Join AB

CHAPTER 3 — REFLECTION

and A'B', and continue these lines until they meet. Where do they meet? (If they do not meet on the paper, choose a fresh pair of points B and B', and try again.)

4 Make an exact copy of Figure 3.5, and find the mirror line under reflection in which P' and Q' are the images of P and Q.

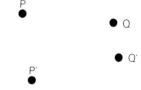

Figure 3.5

5 Trace the pairs of figures in Figure 3.6 and for each pair find the mirror line under reflection in which each figure is the image of the other.

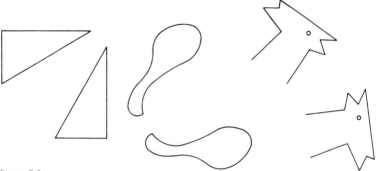

Figure 3.6

6 Plot each of the following pairs of points, and for each pair draw the mirror line of the reflection which maps each of the pair onto the other.

a (−3, 5), (3, 5)   c (2, 3), (−2, −3)   e (0, 0), (6, 6)
b (1, 4), (4, 1)   d (2, 1), (2, 7)   f (4, 4), (0, 8)

7 In Figure 3.7, name the mirror lines of the reflections which map triangle OAB onto each of the following triangles:

a OCB   c OED
b OAH   d OGF

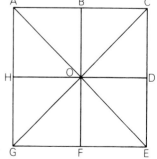

Figure 3.7

8 In Figure 3.7, name the mirror lines of the reflections which map triangle AOC onto each of the following triangles:

a EOC   b GOE   c AOE   d COA

9 What kind of figure can be mapped onto itself by reflection in some mirror line? What is this mirror line then called?

The notation of transformation geometry

As transformations (including reflection) are mappings, the notation for a transformation is the same as that for any other mapping, except that capital letters are normally used for transformations. Thus, if *T* denotes reflection in a line l, then *T*(A) is the image of A under reflection in l, *T*(ABC) is the image of triangle ABC under the same reflection, and so on.

Example 1 In Figure 3.8, *U*, *V*, *W*, *X*, *Y* and *Z* are the names of the six triangles. *P* denotes reflection in line l, *Q* reflection in line m, and *R* reflection in line n. Name

   a *P*(*U*)   **b** *Q*(*Z*)

Also fill in the gaps in

   c *R*( ) = *V*   **d** (*Y*) = *X*

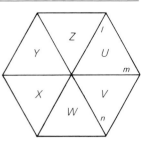

Figure 3.8

Answer

   a *P*(*U*) = *Z*   **b** *Q*(*Z*) = *W*   **c** *R*(*W*) = *V*   **d** *Q*(*Y*) = *X*

Exercise 3.3

1 With the figure and notation of Example 1, above, name

   a *P*(*W*)   **c** *R*(*Y*)   **e** *Q*(*X*)
   b *Q*(*V*)   **d** *P*(*V*)   **f** *R*(*U*)

2 With the figure and notation of Example 1, fill in the gaps in

   a *P*( ) = *U*   **c** *R*( ) = *Z*   **e** (*V*) = *U*
   b *Q*( ) = *X*   **d** (*Y*) = *V*   **f** (*X*) = *W*

3 *X* denotes reflection in the *x*-axis, *Y* reflection in the *y*-axis, and *T* reflection in the line $x = y$. A is (2, 3) and B is (−2, 5). Give the coordinates of

   a *X*(A)   **c** *T*(A)   **e** *Y*(A)
   b *Y*(B)   **d** *X*(B)   **f** *T*(B)

4 *X*, *Y* and *T* have the same meanings as in Question 3. C is (3, 0), D is (0, 3), E is (3, 3). Give the coordinates of

   a *X*(C)   **c** *Y*(E)   **e** *T*(D)
   b *X*(D)   **d** *Y*(C)   **f** *T*(E)

CHAPTER 3 — REFLECTION

5 P, Q, R and S denote reflections in the four sides of a square. O is a point inside the square. What kind of figure is formed by P(O), Q(O), R(O) and S(O), if O is **a** the centre of the square, **b** any point on a diagonal of the square, **c** any point on the perpendicular bisector of a side of the square?

6 W, X, Y and Z denote reflections in the four sides of a quadrilateral, and P is the point where the diagonals of the quadrilateral intersect. What sort of figure is formed by W(P), X(P), Y(P) and Z(P) if the original quadrilateral is

    a a parallelogram   **b** a rectangle   **c** a rhombus?

7 L and M denote reflections in two parallel lines which are 5 cm apart. P is a point between the lines and 2 cm from one of them. Calculate the distance between L(P) and M(P). Repeat the calculation taking P as being 1 cm from one of the lines, instead of 2 cm.

8 Repeat Question 7, but take the distance from P to one of the lines as x cm. Hence show that the distance between L(P) and M(P) is the same for all positions of P. What happens if P is not between the two lines?

9 T is a triangle and P, Q, R denote reflections in the three sides.

    a If the figure formed by T and P(T) is an isosceles triangle, what kind of triangle is T? What are the figures formed by T and Q(T) and by T and R(T) in this case?
    b If the figure formed by T, P(T), Q(T) and R(T) is a triangle, what kind of triangle is T?

10 Draw a circle, mark three points on it A, B and C and draw the triangle ABC. (The points should be chosen so that ABC is an acute-angled triangle.) U, V and W denote reflections in BC, CA and AB respectively. Find U(A) and join this point to A: where the joining line crosses the circle, name this point K. Find U(K) and name it H. Find V(H) and W(H). What do you notice about these points?

Chapter 4
Composite mappings and functions

In the wedding-group, the bride's name is Alice, and she is now the wife of Mr Ash. Her mother's name is Mrs Beech. So Mrs Beech is the mother of the wife of Mr Ash: this is a **composite** relation, though often referred to by a single expression, 'is the mother-in-law of'.

In terms of mappings if $w: x \to$ wife of x,
and $m: x \to$ mother of x, then
Alice = w(Mr Ash),
Mrs Beech = m(Alice)
= m(w(Mr Ash)),

but we can do without the outer brackets and write
Mrs Beech = mw(Mr Ash).

So mw:$x \to$mother of wife of x, or mother-in-law of x. This is a *composite mapping*, and is also a *composite function*.

For the mapping w as defined above, the domain set must obviously be a set of men: for a domain set of men and women we could define s:$x \to$wife or husband of x, and this mapping is used in the following example.

Example 1

If m and s have the meanings defined above, who is the image of Alice Ash under each of these mappings,

a ms   **b** sm   **c** mm   **d** ss?

Answer

a s(Alice) = Mr Ash, so ms(Alice) = m(Mr Ash) = Mrs Ash senior, Alice's mother-in-law.
b m(Alice) = Mrs Beech, so sm (Alice) = Mr Beech.
c mm(Alice) = m(Mrs Beech) = Alice's grandmother.
d ss(Alice) = Mr Ash's wife, that is, Alice herself.

Exercise 4.1

1 If the domain set is {members of a family} c: $x \to$child of x, and b: $x \to$brother or sister of x, what relation to x is

  a cb(x)   **d** bb(x), if x has only one brother or sister
  b bc(x)   **e** bb(x), if x has more than one brother or sister?
  c cc(x)

2 If the domain set is {days of the week}, n: $x \to$day after x, and t: $x \to$the day which is as many days after x as x is after Sunday (so that t(Monday) = Tuesday, t(Wednesday) = Saturday, and so on), what day is

  a nt(Tuesday)   **b** tn(Tuesday)   **c** nn(Tuesday)   **d** tt(Tuesday)?

Find composite mappings that map

  e Thursday onto Saturday   **f** Wednesday onto Sunday,
  g Monday onto Thursday

3 The domain set is {A, B, C, D} and the mappings f and g are defined as follows: f maps A, B, C and D onto B, C, D and A respectively.
       g maps A, B, C and D onto A, D, C and B respectively.
Find fg(A), gf(A), fg(B), gf(B), ff(C) and gg(D).

4 The domain set is {north, north-east, east, south-east, south, south-west, west, north-west}. h maps any direction x onto the direction opposite to x, while k maps any direction x onto the point half-way between x and north (north onto north, south onto east). What are

  a hk(east)   **b** kh(east)   **c** kk(south)   **d** hh(north-west)?

5   A ·   B ·   C ·

    D ·   E ·   F ·

    G ·   H ·   I ·

The domain set consists of the points A to I in the diagram: they form the vertices of nine congruent squares.
p: x→next point below x
q: x→point half-way between x and A.

What points are

a pq(I)   b qp(D)   c pp(B)   d pq(C)?

Find composite mappings that map

e G onto G   f F onto E   g C onto I.

Numerical cases

Composite mappings can be built up from simple ones in numerical cases, in exactly the same way as in the non-numerical cases of the previous section.

Example 2 If f:x→x−3 and g:x→5x, find fg(3), gf(3), ff(3) and gg(3).

Answer
g(3) = 15, so fg(3) = f(15) = 12 and gg(3) = 5 × 15 = 75
f(3) = 0, so gf(3) = g(0) = 0 and ff(3) = f(0) = −3

Exercise 4.2

1 If f:x→3x, g:x→x+2 and h:x→¼x, find

   a fg(6)   c fh(6)   e gh(6)   g ff(6)   i hh(6)
   b gf(6)   d hf(6)   f hg(6)   h gg(6)

2 If p:x→4−x, q:x→2x, r:x→x^2, find

   a pq(5)   c pr(5)   e qr(5)   g pp(5)   i rr(5)
   b qp(5)   d rp(5)   f rq(5)   h qq(5)

3 If t:x→12/x and u:x→x/12, find

   a tu(4)   b ut(4)   c tt(4)   d uu(4)

4 If f, g and h have the same meanings as in Question 1, find

   a fgh(8)   c fhg(−6)   e ghf(−2)   g fgf(⅔)
   b gfh(4)   d hgf(0)   f hfg(28)

5 If p, q and r have the same meanings as in Question 2, find

   a pqr(−2)   c qrp(6)   e rpr(−1)   g qrr(½)
   b rqp(4)   d pqp(9)   f qqp(7)

6 If t and u have the same meanings as in Question 3, find

a tut(3)   **c** ttu(6)   **e** tuu(12)   **g** ttt(−1)
b utu(3)   **d** utt(12) **f** uut($\tfrac{1}{2}$)

7 If s:$x \to x^2$ and f:$x \to$ largest prime factor of x, find sf(12), fs(12), sf(13), and fs(13).
Write out each of the following sentences with the gap filled by the correct word chosen from 'all', 'some' and 'no'.
fs(x) = sf(x) for ––– values of x.
fs(x) = f(x) for ––– values of x.
sf(x) is a prime number for ––– values of x.
Give a brief reason for each answer.

8 If s:$x \to x^2$ and r:$x \to$ remainder when x is divided by 4, find r(8), r(9), r(10), sr(8), sr(9), sr(10), rs(8), rs(9) and rs(10).
Write out the following sentences, each with the gap filled by the correct word chosen from 'all', 'some' and 'no'.
r(x) = rs(x) for ––– values of x.
rs(x) ∈ {0, 1} for ––– values of x.
sr(x) < 10 for ––– values of x.
Give a brief reason for each answer.

9 The function f maps any integer n onto the number of letters of its name in English: thus f(2) = 3 because the word 'two' has three letters. Write down the values of f(3), ff(3) and fff(3). Show that if any integer n is repeatedly mapped by f, the result will eventually come to one particular number, and stay at that number however often the mapping is repeated. What is this number? (It may be assumed that f(n) < n if n > 10.) Show that the result is of a different kind if the **French** names of the numbers are used, and explain why this is so.

10 For the domain set of positive integers, the mapping g is defined as follows:

If n is even, g(n) = $\tfrac{1}{2}n$.
If n is odd, g(n) = $n+1$.

Write down the values of g(7), g(8), gg(7) and gg(8). Investigate what happens when any integer is repeatedly mapped by g.

Composition of algebraic mappings

A composite mapping made up from simple algebraic mappings, like those in Questions 1 to 6 of Exercise 4.2, can be expressed as a single mapping by applying the ordinary processes of algebra. This is best understood by studying the following examples.

Example 3   If $f: x \to x - 3$ and $g: x \to 5x$, express ff, gg, fg and gf as single mappings.

Answer
$ff: x \to (x - 3) - 3 = x - 6$
$gg: x \to 5(5x) = 25x$
$fg: x \to 5x - 3$ (Note that, as always, the second-named mapping, g, is performed first.)
$gf: x \to 5(x - 3) = 5x - 15$

Example 4   Find simple mappings p, q and r such that $pqr: x \to \dfrac{3x + 7}{4}$.

Answer
In this mapping x is first multiplied by 3, then the result is added to 7, and then the result is divided by 4. So the mapping first performed is multiplication by 3, and $r: x \to 3x$.
The mapping performed second is addition to 7, and $q: x \to x + 7$.
The mapping performed third is division by 4, and $p: x \to \tfrac{1}{4}x$.

Exercise 4.3

1 If $f: x \to 3x$, $g: x \to x + 2$ and $h: x \to \tfrac{1}{4}x$, express as single mappings

   a fg   **c** fh   **e** gh   **g** ff   **i** hh
   b gf   **d** hf   **f** hg   **h** gg

2 If $p: x \to 4 - x$, $q: x \to 2x$ and $r: x \to x^2$, express as single mappings

   a pq   **c** pr   **e** qr   **g** pp   **i** rr
   b qp   **d** rp   **f** rq   **h** qq

3 If $t: x \to 12/x$ and $u: x \to x/12$, express as single mappings

   a tu   **b** ut   **c** tt   **d** uu

4 If f, g and h have the same meanings as in Question 1, express as single mappings

   a fgh   **c** fhg   **e** ghf   **g** fgf
   b gfh   **d** hgf   **f** hfg

5 If p, q and r have the same meanings as in Question 2, express as single mappings

   a pqr   **c** qrp   **e** rpr   **g** qrr
   b rqp   **d** pqp   **f** qqp

6 If t and u have the same meanings as in Question 3, express as single mappings

   a tut   **c** ttu   **e** tuu   **g** ttt
   b utu   **d** utt   **f** uut

7 Find simple mappings d, e and f such that $def:x \to \dfrac{3x-2}{7}$. Express as single mappings fed, efd and dfe.

8 Find simple mappings u, v and w such that $uvw:x \to (2x-5)^2$. Express as single mappings wvu, vwu and wuv.

9 Find simple mappings h, k and l such that $hkl:x \to \dfrac{1}{7x+4}$. Express as single mappings klh, lhk and khl.

10 If f, g and h have the same meanings as in Question 1, find values of x which satisfy the following equations:

  a $fg(x) = 9$,   **c** $fh(x) = 6$,   **e** $gh(x) = 1$,
  b $gf(x) = 9$,   **d** $hf(x) = 6$,   **f** $hg(x) = 1$

11 If $m:x \to x+3$, $n:x \to x^2$ and $p:x \to x+2$, show that $pnm:x \to x^2+6x+11$, and hence find the two values of x for which $x^2+6x+11 = 27$.

12 If $r:x \to x-1$, $s:x \to x^2$ and $t:x \to x+1$, express tsr as a single mapping in its simplest form, and hence find the two values of x for which $x^2-2x+2 = 2$.

13 If $g:x \to x+2$ and $h:x \to \dfrac{12}{x}$, express gh and hg as single mappings. What values of x, if any, must be omitted from the domains of

  a g   **b** h   **c** gh   **d** hg?

14 If $d:x \to 5-x$ and $e:x \to \sqrt{x}$, express de and ed as single mappings. What sets of values of x, if any, must be omitted from the domains of

  a d   **b** e   **c** de   **d** ed?

Chapter 5
Rotation

Rotation is another kind of transformation: in Figure 5.1, the flag A'B'C' is the image of the flag ABC under a rotation of +40° about the centre O. (It is customary to regard clockwise rotations as negative, anticlockwise ones as positive.)

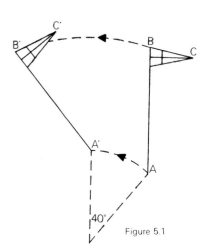

Figure 5.1

Drawing the image In order to draw the image of a given figure under a rotation of, say, 40° about a centre O, begin by drawing two lines, OP and OQ, through O so that the angle POQ is 40°. On a piece of tracing paper trace the figure, the point O and the line OP. Hold the tracing paper down at O by means of a compass-point or ball-point tip, and

turn it until the tracing of OP fits over OQ. Then press the figure through onto the drawing paper.

When coordinates are used and the angle is a multiple of 90° it is often possible to locate and draw the image directly, without the use of tracing paper, and this should be done whenever possible, as in the following example.

Example 1 Draw the image of the flag ABC under

a a rotation of −90° about (0, 0)
b a rotation of 180° about (−1, 0)
c a rotation of +90° about (2, 3)

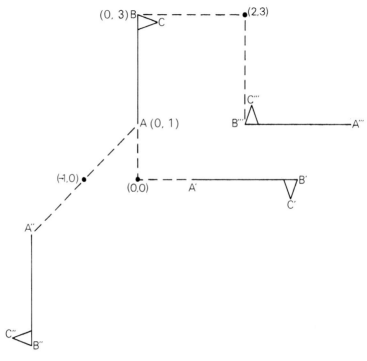

Figure 5.2

Answer
a This is easily seen to be the flag A'B'C' in the diagram.
b This requires a little more thought: it is sometimes helpful to join the centre of rotation to a point of the figure, as shown by the dotted lines: the image is A"B"C".
c As with b: the image is A'''B'''C'''

Exercise 5.1

1 Copy Figure 5.3 and draw the image of the flag under rotation about A

   a of +45°   **b** of +120°   **c** of −90°

2 Make a fresh copy of Figure 5.3 and repeat Question 1, but with B as the centre of rotation.

3 Mameka fresh copy of Figure 5.3 and repeat Question 1, but with C as the centre of rotation.

Figure 5.3

4 Plot the points A (3, 1), B (1, 6) and C (−1, 4) and join them to form a triangle. Use tracing paper to draw the image of this triangle under rotation about (0, 0) of

   a 60°   **b** −45°   **c** 135°

5 Repeat question 4, but with (3, 2) as the centre of rotation.

6 Plot the points D(0, −1), E(1, 2) and F(−1, 1) and join them to form a triangle. Draw the image of this triangle under rotation about D of

   a 50°   **b** −120°   **c** 170°

7 Repeat Question 6, but with (0, 1) as centre of rotation.

8 Plot the same points as for Question 4. Without using tracing paper, draw the image of triangle ABC under rotation about (0, 0) of

   a 90°   **b** 180°   **c** −90°

9 Plot the same points as for Question 6. Without using tracing paper, draw the image of triangle DEF under rotation about (1, 0) of

   a 90°   **b** 180°   **c** −90°

10 Find expressions for the image of (p, q) under rotation about (0, 0) of

   a 90°   **b** 180°   **c** −90°

11 With (0, 0) as centre, find the angles of the rotations that map (5, 0) onto

   a (3, 4)   **c** (0, 5)   **e** (−5, 0)   **g** (0, −5)
   b (4, 3)   **d** (−3, 4)   **f** (−3, −4)

CHAPTER 5 — ROTATION

12 With (2, 3) as centre, find the angles of the rotations that map (6, 6) onto

a (5, 7)
b (2, 8)
c (−2, 6)
d (−2, 0)
e (5, −1)

13 Copy the figure of Question 13 in Exercise 3.1 of Chapter 3. At the end of the over, the field has to change to its image under a rotation of 180° about a point midway between the wickets. Draw in colour the fielders' positions after this change, and repeat the last part of Question 13 in Exercise 3.1, as applied to this transformation.

14 Repeat Question 13, but with reference to the state of affairs when, at the end of the over, a left-handed batsman, instead of a right-handed one, faces the bowling.

Finding the centre (1)

When a figure and its image under a rotation are given, it is often possible to find, simply by inspection, the centre and angle of the rotation involved. If there is any doubt about the answer, it can be checked by the use of tracing paper.

Exercise 5.2

1 Give the centres and angles of the rotations that map rectangle P in Figure 5.4 onto

a rectangle Q
b rectangle R
c rectangle S

Give the image of B in each case.

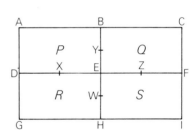

Figure 5.4

2 Give the centre and angles of the rotations that map

a Q onto P
b Q onto R
c Q onto S
d R onto S

Give the image of E in each case.

3 Give the centres and angles of three different rotations that map triangle W onto triangle X in Figure 5.5. Name the image of J in each case.

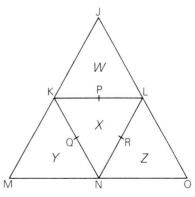

Figure 5.5

4 Give the centres and angles of two different rotations that map W onto Y. Name the image of J in each case.

5 Repeat Question 4, but mapping W onto Z.

6 Plot the points O(0, 0), A(3, 0), B(0, 3) and C(0, 6). Find the coordinates of the centres and the angles of the rotations that map

    a A onto B and O onto C   **b** A onto C and O onto B

7 Plot the points O(0, 0), P(2, 6), Q(0, 4) and R(−6, 6). Show that a certain rotation with centre (−2, 2) will map O onto Q and P onto R, and find the angle of this rotation. Find the centre and angle of a rotation that will map O onto R and P onto Q.

8 Find the centres and angles of the rotations that map (0, 0) and (0, 2) respectively onto

    a (0, 0) and (2, 0)   **c** (2, 2) and (2, 0)
    b (2, 0) and (0, 0)   **d** (−2, −2) and (0, −2)

9 Find the centres of several rotations that would map A(−4, 0) onto B(4, 0). Do these centres lie on a straight line? If so, what straight line is it? What is the relation between this line and AB?

10 Repeat Question 9 but replacing A and B by C(5, 0) and D(0, 5).

Finding the centre (2)

In less simple cases, the centre of rotation cannot easily be found by inspection, and Questions 9 and 10 in the above exercise give the clue to the procedure which has to be adopted.

Choose any point A in the figure, and find its image point A'. Using the results of Questions 9 and 10 above, draw the line of centres of the rotations that map A onto A'.

Choose another point B and find its image point B'. In the same way as before, draw the line of centres of the rotations that map B onto B'.

The point where these two lines intersect is the centre of a rotation that will map A onto A' and also B onto B': it will therefore map the whole figure onto the required image.

Exercise 5.3

1 Draw line-segments PQ and RS, each 5 cm long, and not parallel. Draw the line of centres of the rotations that map P onto R. Draw the line of centres of the rotations that map Q onto S. If these lines of centres intersect on your paper, mark their point of intersection O; if they do not, start again with two different line-segments. Use tracing paper to verify that O is the centre of the rotation that maps PQ onto RS. Why was it specified that PQ and RS must not be parallel? Draw the lines OP and OR, and hence measure the angle of the rotation.

2   Copy each of the pairs of figures in Figure 5.6, and in each case find the centre of the rotation that maps the shaded figure onto the unshaded one. Find also the angle of each rotation.

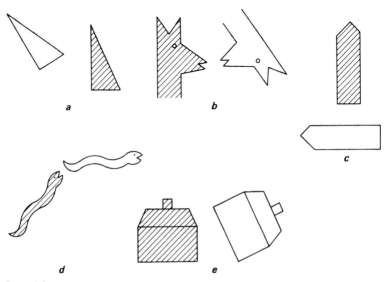

Figure 5.6

3   A is (2, 0), B is (4, 0), C is (4, 1). Find the centres and angles of the rotations that map A, B and C in that order onto each of the following sets of points

   a (2, 2), (2, 4), (1, 4)   **c** (4, −6), (4, −4), (3, −4)
   b (−6, 2), (−8, 2), (−8, 1)

4   O is (0, 0), P is (5, 0) and Q is (5, −2). For each of the following pairs of points, find the centre and angle of the rotation that maps O onto the first and P onto the second, and in each case find the coordinates of the image of Q.

   a (3, 1), (6, 5)   **b** (0, 4), (−3, 8)   **c** (−5, 5), (−1, 2)

5   Draw any figure, trace it onto tracing paper and use this to make a copy of your figure on the same piece of paper as the original, but tilted with respect to it. Find the centre of the rotation that maps the original figure onto the copy, and use your tracing paper to verify the result.

Notation for transformations

As transformations are mappings, the same notation is used for transformations as for mappings, except that transformations are usually denoted by capital letters.

So if R denotes a rotation of 40° about O (see Figure 5.7), $R(P)$ denotes the image of P under R, whether P is a single point or, as in the diagram, a whole figure.

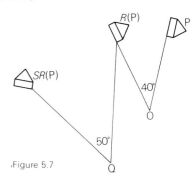

Figure 5.7

Composition of transformations

If a figure (or point) P is transformed by a transformation R and the image $R(P)$ is then transformed by a second transformation S, the image under this second transformation is denoted by $SR(P)$. SR is then a composite transformation, though it may be equivalent to a simple one.

In Figure 5.7, S is a rotation of 50° about the point Q, and $SR(P)$ is the image of $R(P)$ under this rotation, and the image of P under SR. It would, however, be possible to find a single rotation under which $SR(P)$ is the image of P: it could be found quite simply by the method of the previous section.

If this single rotation which maps P onto $SR(P)$ is called U, we can write $U(P)=SR(P)$, and in general $U=SR$, as U will be equivalent to R followed by S whatever the figure being transformed is. For brevity, RR can be written R^2, RRR can be written R^3 and so on.

Example 2

L and M denote rotations of 90° about the points (3, 0) and (−3, 0) respectively (Figure 5.8). Find the images of O(0, 0) under

  a L **b** ML **c** L^2

Answer

a $L(O)$ is the result of rotating O through 90° about (3, 0), and is seen in the diagram to be (3, −3).

b $ML(O)$ is the result of rotating $L(O)$, which has just been shown to be (3, −3) through 90° about (−3, 0), and is seen in the figure to be (0, 6).

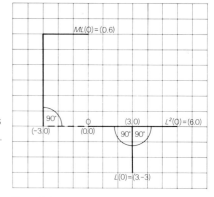

Figure 5.8

c $L^2(O)$ is the result of rotating $L(O)$, i.e. (3, −3), through another 90° about (3, 0): it is seen in the figure to be (6, 0).

Exercise 5.4

1 R and S denote rotations of −90° about (0, 0) and (0, 5) respectively, and P is (3, 2). Give the coordinates of

    a R(P)   **c** SR(P)   **e** $S^2(P)$ **g** $R^3(P)$
    b $R^2(P)$ **d** S(P)   **f** RS(P)   **h** $S^4(P)$

2 Draw the triangle T whose vertices are (3, 0), (3, 2) and (4, 2). If H and K denote rotations of 90° about (0, 0) and (0, 2) respectively, draw KH(T) and HK(T). Find the centres and angles of the single rotations equivalent to KH and to HK.

3 Copy Figure 5.9 full size. X and Y denote rotations of 40° about O and P respectively. Use tracing paper to draw the images of the flag F under the following:

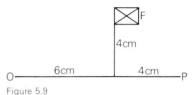

Figure 5.9

    a X   **b** YX   **c** Y   **d** XY   **e** X^2Y

Find the centres and angles of the single rotations equivalent to YX, XY and X^2Y, and verify your results with tracing paper.

4 Draw the triangle U whose vertices are (2, 0), (4, 0) and (2, 1). If R and S denote rotations of 45° about (5, 0) and (0, 5) respectively, draw RS(U) and SR(U). Find the centres and angles of the single rotations equivalent to RS and to SR.

5 If U and T denote rotations of 60° and 100° respectively about the same point O, describe the rotations denoted by

    a UT   **c** T^2 **e** TUT^2
    b TU   **d** UTU

If U^n leaves a figure in its original position, what is the smallest possible value of n?
If T^m leaves a figure in its original position, what is the smallest possible value of m?
If $U^p = T^q$, what are the smallest possible values of p and q?

6 Draw a triangle ABC with AC = BC and C a right angle, and A, B, C in clockwise order. Draw the image of ABC under a rotation of 90° about A, and the image of this image under a rotation of 90° about the *original* position of B. Name the centre and angle of the single rotation that is equivalent to these two rotations.

Repeat the above, but with both rotations through angles of −90°. Name the angle of the equivalent single rotation, and describe its centre in relation to A, B and C.

7 Draw an equilateral triangle XYZ with X, Y, Z in clockwise order. Draw the image of XYZ under a rotation of 60° about X, and the image of this image under a rotation of 60° about the *original* position of Y. Name the angle and describe the centre of the single rotation which maps X, Y and Z respectively onto the same three points as the double rotation does. Repeat the above, but with both rotations through angles of −60°.

8 Repeat Question 7, but with rotations of 120° instead of 60°.

Rotation and reflection

The previous exercise dealt only with rotations. This exercise deals also with the composition of reflections, both with each other and with rotations.

Exercise 5.5

1 X denotes reflection in the x-axis, Y reflection in the y-axis, and R reflection in the line $x = y$. A is (2, 3) and B is (−2, 5). Give the coordinates of

a $XY(A)$
b $YR(A)$
c $RX(A)$
d $YX(B)$
e $RY(B)$
f $XR(B)$
g $XYR(A)$
h $YRX(B)$
i $RXY(A)$
j $XRX(A)$
k $X^2Y^2(B)$

2 Draw a set of parallel lines 2 cm apart. Denote reflections in successive lines by R_1, R_2, R_3 etc. Draw any simple figure T which cuts the first line but none of the others. Draw $R_1(T)$, $R_2R_1(T)$, $R_3R_2R_1(T)$ and so on, forming a pattern.

3 Repeat Question 2 but with T crossing the first *two* of the lines.

4 Repeat Question 2 but instead of using parallel lines, use lines which all pass through a point, each making an angle of 30° with the previous one.

5 In this question, X, Y and R have the same meanings as in Question 1. Draw a 'flag' F by plotting and joining the points (5, 1), (5, 2), (6, 2) and (6, 1).
By drawing $X(F)$ and $YX(F)$, find the single transformation equivalent to YX.
By drawing $Y(F)$ and $XY(F)$, find the single transformation equivalent to XY.
What do your answers suggest is the result of combining two reflections?

CHAPTER 5 — ROTATION

6 Copy Figure 5.10 on a larger scale, making all the acute angles 60°. The exact position of the face G does not matter. Let P denote reflection in AOB and let denote reflection in AOB and let Q denote QP(G), Q(G) and PQ(G). Name the single transformations which are equivalent to QP and to PQ. Without any more drawing, name the single transformations which are equivalent to QPQP and PQPQ.

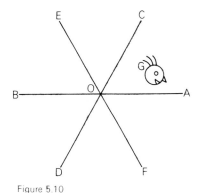

Figure 5.10

7 With the same notation as in Question 5, draw XYR(F) and express XYR as a single transformation. Similarly find the single transformations equivalent to XRY, YRX, YXR and RYX.

8 With the figure and notation of Question 6, draw PQP(G) and QPQ(G). Name the single transformations equivalent to PQP and to QPQ.

9 With the figure and notation of Question 6, and also with R denoting reflection in EOF, find the single transformations equivalent to PQR, PRQ, RPQ and RQP.

10 In Figure 5.11, angle LOM=40° and angle POL=10°. P' is the image of P under reflection in OM: calculate angles P'OM and P'OL. P" is the image of P' under reflection in OL: calculate angles P"OL and POP". Through what angle has P been rotated about O by the double reflection? Repeat the question with angle POM 15° instead of 10°. What conclusion does this suggest?

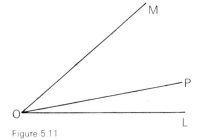

Figure 5.11

11 With the figure of Question 10, take angle POM as $x°$ instead of 10°, and find expressions for angles P'OM, P'OL, P"OL and POP".
Repeat the above with angle LOM taken as $y°$ instead of 40°. What do your results prove?

12 In Questions 6 and 7, investigate the effect if P is reflected first in OL and then in OM.

13 Investigate whether it is possible for the combined effect of two reflections to be anything other than a rotation.

Chapter 6
Large and small numbers

The astronomer in the picture may be looking at a star whose distance from the earth is

240 000 000 000 000 km

but with more powerful telescopes it is possible to see galaxies as far away as

10 000 000 000 000 000 000 000 km.

The biologist may be looking at a creature whose diameter is 0.0003 cm, but with an electron microscope he could see an object of diameter 0.000 000 1 cm. And a physicist may be dealing with particles millions of times smaller than that.

The method of writing very large and very small numbers out in full, with many 0's, is wasteful of time and space and can easily lead to serious

CHAPTER 6 — LARGE AND SMALL NUMBERS

errors. Instead of writing out in full the first number written above, we could write it

$$24 \times 10^{13} \quad \text{or} \quad 2.4 \times 10^{14}.$$

The second of the above two versions of the number illustrates the method most often used: it is called *standard form* (or sometimes 'scientific notation', especially by the makers of calculators). When this method is used, the first number (which we shall call the *leading number*) always lies between 1 and 10, so that the decimal point, if there is one, comes after the first digit. The leading number can be 1, but it cannot be 10. Any number of any size can be put into standard form, but it is particularly useful with very large and very small numbers.

At first we shall deal only with large numbers. It will be seen that the index of 10 is simply the number of figures (mainly zeros) between the position of the decimal point when the number is written out in full, and its position in standard form.

Exercise 6.1

1 Write the following numbers in standard form.

   a 25 000
   b 2 160 000
   c 234 000 000
   d 985 000 000 000
   e 6 184 000 000
   f 72 100 000 000
   g 123×10^3
   h 34×10^7
   i 8932×10^9

2 Write in figures in standard form.

   a twenty-three thousand
   b six million, two hundred and thirty thousand
   c forty-seven million
   d two hundred and thirty-nine million
   e seventeen thousand million
   f eighty-four million million
   g nine million million million

3 Find, giving answers in standard form,

   a the number of centimetres in 37 km
   b the number of milligrams in 0.47 kg
   c the number of millimetres in 473 m
   d the number of grams in 37 tonnes
   e the number of square centimetres in 4.3 m^2
   f the number of cubic centimetres in 88 litres
   g the number of cubic centimetres in 10 cubic metres

4 Another way of expressing very large numbers is by the use of very large units: just as the prefix kilo- denotes 1000 of the basic unit (so that 1 km = 1000 m), so

mega- denotes 1 million or 10^6 of the basic unit,
giga- denotes 1 thousand million or 10^9,
tera- denotes 1 million million or 10^{12}.

Express in standard form

a 23 megohms in ohms
b 0.7 gigawatts in watts
c 0.034 terajoules in joules

5 Write out in full the following numbers.

a 2.4×10^4 **c** 8.04×10^5 **e** 8.349×10^5
b 3.62×10^6 **d** 7×10^7 **f** 2.345×10^2

6 Express

a 6×10^7 mm in metres **d** 5.34×10^4 m in kilometres
b 3.6×10^6 g in kilograms **e** 2.08×10^8 g in tonnes
c 7.8×10^5 cm³ in litres **f** 9.56×10^9 m² in sq km

Multiplication and division of numbers in standard form

The leading numbers are multiplied or divided in the usual way, and the powers of 10 are multiplied by adding the indices or divided by subtracting the indices.

Example 1 Multiply 3.1×10^6 by 2.2×10^5

Answer
$3.1 \times 2.2 = 6.82$, and $6 + 5 = 11$, so the product is 6.82×10^{11}

Example 2 Multiply 8.4×10^3 by 2.5×10^7

Answer
$8.4 \times 2.5 = 21$, and $3 + 7 = 10$, so the product is 21×10^{10} but this is not in standard form as $21 > 10$. We must write $21 = 2.1 \times 10$, and the product is $2.1 \times 10 \times 10^{10} = 2.1 \times 10^{11}$.

Example 3 Divide 1.32×10^9 by 1.1×10^6.

Answer
$1.32 \div 1.1 = 1.2$, and $9 - 6 = 3$, so the quotient is 1.2×10^3.

Exercise 6.2

Give all answers in standard form.

1. If $x = 1.6 \times 10^3$, $y = 2.4 \times 10^4$ and $z = 4.8 \times 10^6$, find the values of

   a xy **c** xz **e** y^2
   b x^2 **d** yz **f** z^2

2. If x, y and z denote the same numbers as in Question 1, find the values of

   a y/x **c** y^2/z **e** zx/y
   b z/x **d** yz/x

3. If $p = 4.32 \times 10^5$, $q = 2.5 \times 10^3$ and $r = 1.01 \times 10^4$, find the values of

   a pq **c** qr **e** pr/q
   b pr **d** p/q **f** pqr

4. Find the area of a rectangle whose length is 8.4×10^3 m and whose breadth is 1.5×10^3 m.

5. The scale of a map is 50 000:1. Express this in standard form. The length and breadth of a rectangular wood are shown on the map as 2.4 cm and 1.8 cm. Find the length and breadth of the actual wood **a** in centimetres, **b** in metres. Find also the area of the wood in square metres.

6. The distance between two villages is 10.6 km. Express this in metres in standard form. Find the distance between the points marking the villages on the map referred to in Question 5, giving the answer in centimetres.

7. A metal casting weighs 3.2×10^4 g. Find the total weight of 4.1×10^3 such castings,

   a in grams   **b** in kilograms   **c** in tonnes

8. A space craft travels at 7.5×10^3 m/s. Find,

   a its speed in kilometres per hour,
   b the time in hours (to 2 significant figures) that it would take to reach the sun, a distance of 1.5×10^8 km.

Small numbers: negative indices

If we have to divide 10^3 by 10^5 and follow the rule for indices, this gives the answer 10^{-2}, which can thus be given a meaning, for we know the answer is in fact 0.01. This gives a clue to the way in which very small numbers can be written in standard form: for example
$0.0003 = 3 \times 0.0001 = 3 \times 10^{-4}$.

Example 4 Put into standard form the numbers $a = 0.000\,012$ and $b = 0.000\,48$; find the value of a/b, expressing it in standard form.

Answer
$a = 1.2 \times 10^{-5}$, $b = 4.8 \times 10^{-4}$
$a/b = (1.2 \div 4.8) \times (10^{-5} \div 10^{-4})$
$\quad = 0.25 \times 10^{(-5-(-4))}$
$\quad = 0.25 \times 10^{-1}$ but 0.25 will not do for a leading number, as it is less than 1. We can write $0.25 = 2.5 \times 10^{-1}$ and $a/b = 2.5 \times 10^{-2}$.

Exercise 6.3

1 Write the following numbers in standard form.

- **a** 0.0046
- **b** 0.000 027
- **c** 0.000 351
- **d** 0.0236
- **e** 0.000 000 020 2
- **f** 0.298
- **g** 0.56×10^{-4}
- **h** 34×10^{-3}
- **i** 0.0345×10^{-6}

2 Write in figures in standard form.

- **a** seven hundredths
- **b** eleven thousandths
- **c** forty-nine ten-thousandths
- **d** twenty-nine millionths
- **e** half a millionth

3 Express in standard form.

- **a** 0.34 m in kilometres
- **b** 17 grams in kilograms
- **c** 23 cm in kilometres
- **d** 347 mg in kilograms
- **e** 0.34 cm³ in litres
- **f** 293 cm³ in cubic metres

4 Another way of expressing very small numbers is by the use of very small units: just as the prefix milli- denotes .001 of the basic unit (so that 1 mg = .001 g), so

micro- denotes .000 001 of the basic unit,
nano- denotes .000 000 001 of the basic unit,
pico- denotes .000 000 000 001 of the basic unit.

Express, in standard form.

- **a** 0.34 microseconds in seconds
- **b** 31 nanometres in metres
- **c** 22 picofarads in farads

5 Write out in full the following numbers.

- **a** 1.2×10^{-3}
- **b** 3.85×10^{-8}
- **c** 5.93×10^{-5}
- **d** 7.49×10^{-6}
- **e** 4.32×10^{-4}
- **f** 4.08×10^{-2}

CHAPTER 6 — LARGE AND SMALL NUMBERS 51

6 If $t=1.2\times10^{-2}$, $u=2.4\times10^{-3}$, $v=4.8\times10^{-5}$, find the values of

a tu **c** tv **e** u^2
b uv **d** t^2 **f** v^2

giving the answers in standard form.

7 If t, u and v denote the same numbers as in Question 6, find the values of

a t/u **c** u/v **e** t/v
b u/t **d** v/u **f** v/t

giving the answers in standard form.

8 If $d=3.2\times10^4$, $e=1.6\times10^{-3}$, $f=6.4\times10^{-5}$, find the values of

a de **c** ef **e** d/f **g** f/d
b df **d** d/e **f** e/d

giving the answers in standard form.

Addition and subtraction of numbers in standard form

1 If the powers of 10 are the same, add or subtract the leading numbers. If the result is more than 10 or less than 1, make the necessary adjustment as in other cases.

Example 5 Find the value of $(8.4\times10^6)+(7.3\times10^6)$.

Answer
$8.4+7.3=15.7$, but 15.7×10^6 is not in standard form: we must write 1.57×10^7.

Example 6 Find the value of $(5.83\times10^5)-(5.81\times10^5)$.

Answer
$5.83-5.81=0.02$, but 0.02×10^5 is not in standard form. Since $0.02=2\times10^{-2}$ the answer is 2×10^3.

2 If the powers of 10 are different, the smaller number must be taken out of standard form and put into a form whose power of 10 is the same as that of the larger number.

Example 7 Find the value of $7.1\times10^5+4.7\times10^4$.

Answer
4.7×10^4 must be rewritten as 0.47×10^5. Then $7.1+0.47=7.57$, so the answer is 7.57×10^5.

Example 8 Find the value of $(8.3 \times 10^{-4}) - (3.1 \times 10^{-5})$.

Answer

3.1×10^{-5} must be rewritten as 0.31×10^{-4}. Then $8.3 - 0.31 = 7.99$, so the answer is 7.99×10^{-4}.

Exercise 6.4 Miscellaneous

Give all answers in standard form when this is suitable.

1 Calculate

   a $(8.6 \times 10^6) + (7.3 \times 10^6)$
   b $(4.7 \times 10^{-5}) + (5.8 \times 10^{-5})$
   c $(5.4 \times 10^7) + (6.3 \times 10^6)$
   d $(9.2 \times 10^{-5}) + (1.9 \times 10^{-4})$

2 Calculate

   a $(2.8 \times 10^4) - (2.65 \times 10^4)$
   b $(7.2 \times 10^{-3}) - (6.7 \times 10^{-3})$
   c $(1.4 \times 10^7) - (8.6 \times 10^6)$
   d $(3.22 \times 10^{-3}) - (2.45 \times 10^{-4})$

3 Evaluate $pq - r^2$

   a when $p = 3.3 \times 10^4$, $q = 1.9 \times 10^6$, $r = 2.5 \times 10^5$
   b when $p = 1.8 \times 10^{-3}$, $q = 2.7 \times 10^{-5}$, $r = 2.2 \times 10^{-4}$

4 Give the number

   a of microseconds   **b** of nanoseconds in 1 hour

   (see Exercise 6.3 Question 4).

5 The wavelength of red light is 4×10^{-7} m. Express this

   a in millimetres   **b** in nanometres

   (see Exercise 6.3, Question 4).
   Repeat the above for the diameter of an atom of gold, 2.88×10^{-10} m.

6 Express in the form $n:1$

   a the ratio of the distance of the nearest star, 4×10^{13} km, to that of the sun, 1.5×10^8 km.
   b the ratio of the distance of the nearest galaxy, 1.6×10^{19} km, to that of the nearest star.

7 Find the ratio of the population of the United States, 2.1×10^8, to that of the United Kingdom, 5.6×10^7.

CHAPTER 6 — LARGE AND SMALL NUMBERS

8 The age of the earth has been estimated to be 8×10^9 years. Taking this as correct, what fraction of this time has occurred since

    a the extinction of the dinosaurs, 6.5×10^7 years ago
    b the beginnings of the human race, taken as 2×10^6 years ago?

9 The areas, in square kilometres, of the countries of the United Kingdom are approximately:

England	1.29×10^{11}
Wales	2.1×10^{10}
Scotland	7.7×10^{10}
N. Ireland	1.3×10^{10}

Calculate

    a the total area
    b the amount by which the area of England exceeds half the total
    c the angles of a pie-chart which might be drawn to illustrate this information.

10 Calculate, in litres, the volume of water that falls on 1 square kilometre of land when 1 centimetre of rain falls (i.e. enough to cover the ground to a depth of 1 cm, if the water did not run away). In a storm 2.5 cm of rain fell on the Greater London area, covering 1.56×10^3 km². Calculate the number of tonnes of water that fell on this area (1 litre of water weighs 1 kg).

11 The velocity of radar waves (like that of light) is about 3×10^8 m/s. Calculate the time taken for a radar pulse to reach an aeroplane at a distance of 6×10^3 m from the apparatus and return to the apparatus again.
During this time the spot on the radar screen has moved 5 cm across the screen. Calculate the velocity of the spot in centimetres per second.

12 The masses of two kinds of atoms are approximately:

Hydrogen	1.66×10^{-24} g
Oxygen	2.66×10^{-23}

Calculate the mass of a molecule of water, which consists of two atoms of hydrogen and one of oxygen.
Approximating the above answer to one significant figure, find the approximate number of molecules in 1 gram of water.

Chapter 7

Matrices

A *matrix* is a set of numbers arranged in rows and columns, like the league table which the football fans in the picture are studying. This table is as follows:

	Played	Won	Drawn	Lost
Rovers	6	2	1	3
Albion	7	4	2	1
Rangers	7	3	1	3

When the set of numbers is written as a matrix, the headings are sometimes omitted and the numbers are enclosed in large brackets. A matrix may be named by a single letter, thus:

$$\mathbf{L} = \begin{pmatrix} 6 & 2 & 1 & 3 \\ 7 & 4 & 2 & 1 \\ 7 & 3 & 1 & 3 \end{pmatrix}$$

CHAPTER 7 — MATRICES

The numbers forming the matrix are called its *elements*.

The *order* of a matrix is the number of its rows and the number of its columns: for example **L**, above, is a 3×4 matrix because it has 3 rows and 4 columns.

The *transpose* of a matrix is the matrix obtained by changing its rows into columns and its columns into rows. The transpose of **L**, named **L'**, is

$$\mathbf{L'} = \begin{pmatrix} 6 & 7 & 7 \\ 2 & 4 & 3 \\ 1 & 2 & 1 \\ 3 & 1 & 3 \end{pmatrix}$$

A matrix with only one row is called a *row matrix*; a matrix with only one column is called a *column matrix*.

In Exercises 7.1 and 7.2 the following matrices are used:

$$\mathbf{A} = \begin{pmatrix} 2 & 1 & 4 \\ 3 & 0 & 5 \end{pmatrix}, \quad \mathbf{B} = \begin{pmatrix} 4 & 3 \\ 1 & 2 \end{pmatrix},$$

$$\mathbf{C} = \begin{pmatrix} 3 & 0 & -1 & 2 \\ 2 & -7 & 0 & 3 \end{pmatrix}, \quad \mathbf{D} = \begin{pmatrix} -1 & 0 & 3 \\ 2 & 5 & -3 \end{pmatrix},$$

$$\mathbf{E} = \begin{pmatrix} 1 & 9 \\ 2 & 5 \\ 3 & 4 \end{pmatrix}, \quad \mathbf{F} = \begin{pmatrix} 1 & 3 & 2 & 4 \\ 4 & 5 & 0 & 6 \end{pmatrix},$$

$$\mathbf{G} = \begin{pmatrix} -2 & 0 \\ -4 & 1 \end{pmatrix}, \quad \mathbf{H} = \begin{pmatrix} 0 & 3 \\ 4 & -2 \\ 7 & -1 \end{pmatrix}$$

Exercise 7.1 Matrices as stores of information

1 Write down the order of each of the matrices **A, B, C, D, E, F, G** and **H** above, and arrange them in pairs so that the two members of each pair have the same order.

2 Form matrices with the following orders:

   a 4×2 **b** 3×1 **c** 1×4 **d** 3×3 **e** 2×5

Which of these is a row matrix? Which is a column matrix? Which might suitably be called a *square matrix*?

3 Alf bought 2 bottles of pop, a packet of chocolate and 4 packets of toffee; Betty bought 3 bottles of pop and 5 packets of toffee. This information is stored in the following matrix.

$$\begin{array}{c} \\ \text{Alf} \\ \text{Betty} \end{array} \begin{array}{ccc} \text{Pop} & \text{Chocolate} & \text{Toffee} \\ \begin{pmatrix} 2 & 1 & 4 \\ 3 & 0 & 5 \end{pmatrix} \end{array}$$

Copy this matrix and add two more rows to give information about Carol, who bought 2 packets of chocolate and 3 of toffee, but no pop, and Don who bought one bottle of pop and 2 packets of chocolate, but no toffee.

4 Form a matrix to store this information: Mr Ash has a dog, two cats and four budgerigars, Mrs Beech has two dogs and a cat, and Miss Fox has four cats and seven budgerigars.

5 Form a matrix to store this information: a tetrahedron has 4 faces, 6 edges and 4 vertices; a cube has 6 faces, 12 edges and 8 vertices; an octahedron has 8 faces, 12 edges and 6 vertices; a dodecahedron has 12 faces, 30 edges and 20 vertices; and an icosahedron has 20 faces, 30 edges and 12 vertices.

6 The word MATHEMATICS has 2 A's, 1 E, 1 I and 8 consonants. Form a 5 × 4 matrix to store this information, and also the corresponding information concerning the words MATRIX, ADDITIVE, INVERSE and EXERCISE.

7
$$\begin{matrix} & 2 & 3 & 5 \\ 60 & (2 & 1 & 1) \end{matrix}$$

This is the first row of a matrix conveying information about the prime factors of various numbers: thus 60 is the product of 2 twos, 1 three and 1 five. Complete the matrix so that it gives the corresponding information about the prime factors of 64, 72, 75, 80, 81 and 90.

8 Suggest sets of information that might be stored by each of the following matrices, and write out the matrices with the appropriate headings:

a A, **b** B, **c** E, **d** F

9 Each of four teams, the reds, whites, blues and greens, played each of the others in a tournament. The results are shown in a matrix **L** which is only partly completed:

$$\begin{matrix} & R & W & B & G \\ \text{Reds} & 0 & 2 & 1 & 0 \\ \text{Whites} & & & 1 & 2 \\ \text{Blues} & & & & 2 \\ \text{Greens} & & & & \end{matrix}$$

The first line shows that the reds beat the whites, drew with the blues, and were beaten by the greens.

a Complete the matrix **L**,

b Form another 4 × 4 matrix **M**, with columns headed 'Played', 'Won', 'Drawn' and 'Lost' to summarise the results of each team's games. Keep your answers to this question, as you will need them in answering a question in the next exercise.

10 Write down the transposes of the matrices **A, B, C, D, E, F, G** and **H**, which are at the beginning of this exercise, and state the order of each. What sort of matrix has the same order as its transpose? What sort of matrix is the transpose of a row matrix?

11 In Question 3, if the matrix is transposed, does it still give the same information as the original matrix? What is the difference in the way this information is presented? Write down the transposes of the matrices given as the answers to Questions 4, 5, 6 and 7, and put in appropriate headings to the rows and columns.

12 Figure 7.1 is a map showing the roads between four towns, Ayton, Beeton, Ceeton and Deeton. A matrix, called the direct route matrix, can be formed to show the numbers of direct routes between each pair of towns: its first row is

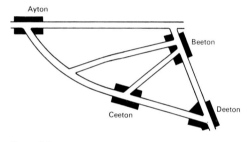

Figure 7.1

$$\begin{array}{cccc} & A & B & C & D \\ A & (0 & 2 & 1 & 0) \end{array}$$

This shows that there are 2 direct routes from Ayton to Beeton, one from Ayton to Ceeton, and no *direct* route from Ayton to Deeton (and of course no route from Ayton to Ayton). Complete this matrix. What can be said about its transpose? Will this be true of the transpose of any direct route matrix?

13 Form the direct route matrix for the five towns on the map in Figure 7.2.

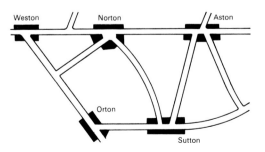

Figure 7.2

14 A matrix can be used to express a relation or mapping. For the mapping illustrated in Figure 7.3, the first row would be

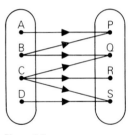

Figure 7.3

$$\begin{array}{ccccc} & P & Q & R & S \\ A & (1 & 0 & 0 & 0) \end{array}$$

because A maps onto P but not onto Q, R or S. Complete the matrix.

15 Draw a mapping diagram for the mapping x→multiple of x between the domain set {2, 3, 5, 7} and the range set {6, 15, 30, 35, 42}. Form the matrix that expresses this mapping.

What mapping is expressed by the transpose of this matrix?

16 Alan is the eldest of four children, of whom Betty is the youngest; the other two are Clara and Denis, who is older than Clara. Draw a diagram for the relation 'is older than', and form the matrix that expresses this relation. What relation is expressed by the transpose of this matrix?

Addition, subtraction and multiplication by a number

Two matrices can be added if and only if they are of the same order. The sum is found by adding corresponding elements of the two matrices.

Subtraction is carried out in a similar way.

A matrix may be multiplied by a number: each element of the matrix is multiplied by that number.

Example 1 If $\mathbf{P} = \begin{pmatrix} 1 & -2 & 5 \\ 4 & 0 & -3 \end{pmatrix}$ and $\mathbf{Q} = \begin{pmatrix} 3 & 1 & 4 \\ 2 & -1 & -5 \end{pmatrix}$, find $\mathbf{P}+\mathbf{Q}$, $\mathbf{P}-\mathbf{Q}$ and $3\mathbf{P}$

Answer

$$\mathbf{P}+\mathbf{Q} = \begin{pmatrix} 1+3 & -2+1 & 5+4 \\ 4+2 & 0+-1 & -3+-5 \end{pmatrix} = \begin{pmatrix} 4 & -1 & 9 \\ 6 & -1 & -8 \end{pmatrix}$$

$$\mathbf{P}-\mathbf{Q} = \begin{pmatrix} 1-3 & -2-1 & 5-4 \\ 4-2 & 0--1 & -3--5 \end{pmatrix} = \begin{pmatrix} -2 & -3 & 1 \\ 2 & 1 & 2 \end{pmatrix}$$

$$3\mathbf{P} = \begin{pmatrix} 3\times1 & 3\times-2 & 3\times5 \\ 3\times4 & 3\times0 & 3\times-3 \end{pmatrix} = \begin{pmatrix} 3 & -6 & 15 \\ 12 & 0 & -9 \end{pmatrix}$$

CHAPTER 7 — MATRICES

Exercise 7.2

1 Add all the pairs of the matrices **A, B, C, D, E, F, G** and **H**, which are at the beginning of Exercise 7.1, that can be added.

2 Subtract all the pairs of the same matrices that can be subtracted (in each case subtracting the second-named from the first).

3 Which of the eight matrices can be added to their own transposes? Carry out these additions.

4 Calculate

    a 2**A**   b 2**B**   c −**C**   d −4**D**   e $\frac{1}{2}$**H**   f −$\frac{1}{2}$**G**

5 The members of forms Upper IVX and Upper IVY are put into two divisions for French and three divisions for mathematics. The matrices which show how each form is allocated are as follows:

UIVX

		Mathematics		
	Division	1	2	3
French	Div. 1	9	6	3
	Div. 2	3	5	5

UIVY

		Mathematics		
	Division	1	2	3
French	Div. 1	5	6	6
	Div. 2	3	7	3

Add the two matrices together. How many are in each division for each subject? How many are in each form?

6 A shop stocks dresses in three sizes, large, medium and small, and in three colours, pink, blue and white.

	Pink	Blue	White
Large	6	8	5
P = Medium	27	32	17
Small	10	4	0

	Pink	Blue	White
Q =	20	20	20
	0	0	10
	20	20	30

	Pink	Blue	White
R =	23	22	19
	20	23	25
	30	19	17

Matrix **P** shows the stock held when the shop closed on a certain Friday, **Q** shows the contents of a delivery made later that evening, and **R** shows the stock held when the shop closed at the end of the next day, Saturday. Find matrices which give the following information:

a the stock held just before opening on Saturday
b the quantities sold during Saturday

Make up a matrix of your own to show the quantities that might have been sold during the following Monday, and from it find another matrix to show the stocks held when the shop closed on Monday.

7 Two model train sets, **A** and **B**, contain rails as given by the following two matrices:

$$\begin{array}{c c c c c} & \text{Straights} & \text{Half-straights} & \text{Curves} & \text{Points} \\ \mathbf{A} = & (2 & 2 & 8 & 0) \\ \mathbf{B} = & (4 & 2 & 12 & 2) \end{array}$$

a Find **B** − **A** and suggest a meaning for it.
b Form a matrix to show the rails needed to make up ten **A** sets and eight **B** sets.

8 The matrix below gives the numbers of lessons in English, mathematics and French attended each week by Ann and Bill.

$$\begin{array}{c c c c} & \text{English} & \text{Mathematics} & \text{French} \\ \text{Ann} & \begin{pmatrix} 5 & 5 & 3 \\ \text{Bill} & 6 & 4 & 2 \end{pmatrix} \end{array}$$

Multiply this matrix by 12 and suggest a meaning for the result.

9 Referring to Question 9 of Exercise 7.1, the four teams played a second round, and in this the reds won all their matches, the greens lost all theirs, and the whites drew with the blues. Form the following matrices:

a **P** which (like **L** in the earlier question) gives the result of each match, but in the second round.
b **Q**, which summarises the results for each team in the second round.
c **L** + **P**, and state what information this gives.
d **Q** + **M**, and state what information this gives.

10 The map (Figure 7.4) shows the roads and footpaths connecting four villages.
Form **R**, the direct route matrix for roads.
Form **F**, the direct route matrix for footpaths.
Form **R** + **F**. What information does it give?

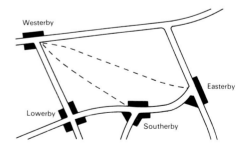

Figure 7.4

11

$$\mathbf{L} = \begin{pmatrix} & \text{Alf} & \text{Bill} & \text{Chris} & \text{Diana} \\ \text{Alf} & 0 & 0 & 0 & 1 \\ \text{Bill} & 0 & 0 & 1 & 0 \\ \text{Chris} & 1 & 0 & 0 & 0 \\ \text{Diana} & 0 & 1 & 0 & 0 \end{pmatrix}$$

The matrix **L** shows the relation 'is next on the left of' between four people sitting round a table.

a Draw a plane to show how the four people are seated,
b Form the matrix **L'** and state what relation it represents,
c Form the matrix **L+L'** and state what relation it represents.

12 Solve the equations.

a $\begin{pmatrix} x & 2 \\ 3 & 7 \end{pmatrix} + \begin{pmatrix} -2 & t \\ u & 5 \end{pmatrix} = \begin{pmatrix} 4 & 1 \\ 7 & 2 \end{pmatrix}$

b $(2x \quad 3 \quad 4) + (2 \quad x \quad -x) = (y \quad y \quad z)$

c $3\begin{pmatrix} x & 2 \\ 1 & 2x \end{pmatrix} = x\begin{pmatrix} 3 & 1 \\ y & z \end{pmatrix}$

d $2\begin{pmatrix} a & b & 4 \\ 3 & e & a \end{pmatrix} + \begin{pmatrix} d & -5 & a \\ 2 & a & 3 \end{pmatrix} = \begin{pmatrix} c & c & b \\ 8 & b & 5 \end{pmatrix}$

13 Solve the following matrix equations, where **A**, **B** etc. have the meanings given above Exercise 7.1, and **W**, **X**, **Y** and **Z** are to be found.

a $2\mathbf{A} + \mathbf{W} = \mathbf{D}$ **b** $\mathbf{B} - \mathbf{X} = 2\mathbf{G}$ **c** $2\mathbf{Y} + \mathbf{H} = \mathbf{E}$ **d** $\mathbf{Z} + \mathbf{C} + \mathbf{F} = \mathbf{O}$

where **O** is a zero matrix, all of whose elements are 0's.

Chapter 8
Translation and vectors

A *translation* is a transformation in which all points of the transformed figure move through the same distance and in the same direction: in other words, the lines joining points to their images are all equal in length, and are all parallel. (See Figure 8.1).

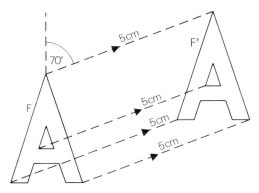

Figure 8.1

CHAPTER 8 — TRANSLATION AND VECTORS

One way to describe a translation is to specify the distance through which the points move, and the direction in which they move: for example, in Figure 8.1 the translation that maps F to F' could be described as a translation of 5 cm in a direction making an angle of 70° with the upward vertical on the paper.

Example 1 In Figure 8.2 all the right-angled triangles are congruent. Name the triangle which is the image of ABE under a translation, and describe the translation.

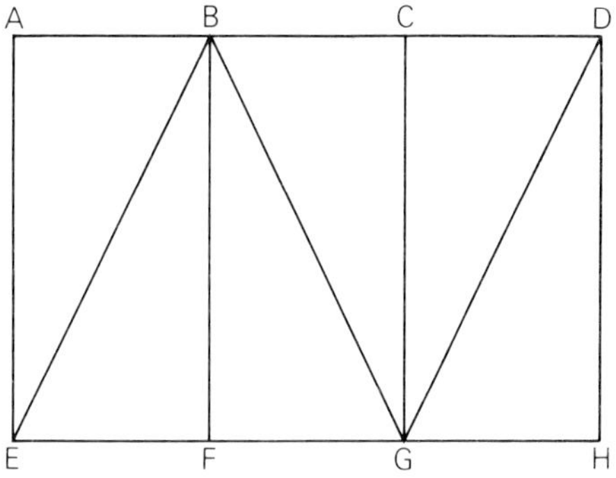

Answer
The only triangle in the figure which is the image of ABE under a *translation* is CDG, since AC, BD and EG are all equal and parallel. The translation is of 4 cm in the direction of AB (or of EF).

Figure 8.2

Exercise 8.1

1. Draw a triangle ABC with AB = 2 cm, AC = 3 cm, and angle BAC = 90°. Draw its image under each of the following translations (in each case starting from the original position of the figure).

   a 2 cm in the direction of AB (i.e. from A towards B)
   b 2 cm in the direction of BA (i.e. the opposite direction from that of **a**)
   c 5 cm in the direction of AC
   d 4 cm in the direction of BC

2. Draw a triangle with the same measurements as that of Question 1. Draw its image under a translation of 4 cm in the direction of AB. Draw the image of this image under a translation of 6 cm in the direction of CA. Describe the single translation that would map triangle ABC onto this second image.

3. On your paper draw lines to represent northerly and easterly directions, as on a map. Draw any simple figure F. If T and U denote translations of 5 cm northward and eastward respectively, draw $T(F)$, $T^2(F)$, $U(F)$ and $U^2(F)$. Describe the single translations that would map

   a $T(F)$ onto $U(F)$ **c** $T^2(F)$ onto $U^2(F)$
   b $U(F)$ onto $T(F)$ **d** $U^2(F)$ onto $T^2(F)$

Also, draw $TU(F)$ and describe the single transformation that would map F onto $TU(F)$.

4 In Figure 8.3, the parallelograms are all congruent. The translation P maps the shaded parallelogram KLPQ onto the dotted parallelogram RSXW. Name the image under P of

a ABGF   c LMRQ,   e triangle FLM
b GHML   d triangle ACP   f parallelogram BHLF

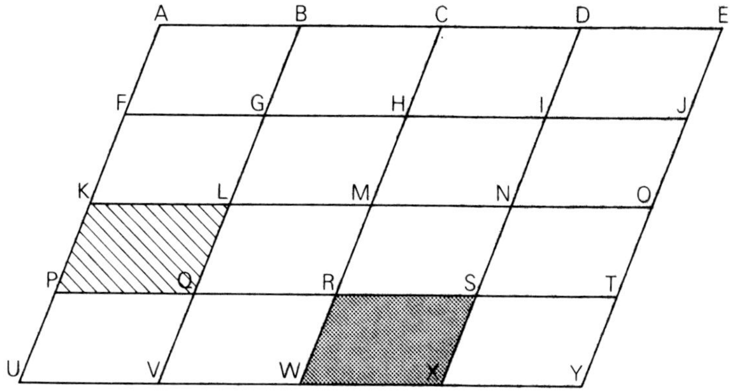

Figure 8.3

5 In Figure 8.3, name the image of the dotted parallelogram under the translation that would map the shaded parallelogram onto

a ABGF   b GHML   c LMRQ

6 O, P and Q are the points (0, 0), (3, 2) and (−1, 3) respectively. A translation T maps O onto (4, −1). Find the coordinates of $T(P)$, $T(Q)$, $T^2(O)$, $T^2(P)$, $T^2(Q)$ and $T^3(O)$.

7 A, B and C are the points (2, 1), (3, 5) and (5, 2). A translation U is such that $U(A) = B$. Find the coordinates of $U(B)$, $U(C)$, $U^2(A)$, $U^2(B)$ and $U^2(C)$.
If $U(C)$ is called D, what sort of figure is ABDC? What is the image of B under a translation that would map A onto C?

8 The translations F and G map (0, 0) onto (4, 5) and (3, −2) respectively. Find the image of (−1, 2) under

a F b G c GF d FG e F^2 f G^2 g F^2G^2

9 Draw a rectangle ABCD with AB = 4 cm, BC = 3 cm. Let the diagonals intersect at O. Draw the image AO'D of triangle AOD under reflection in AD. Draw the image A"O"D" of AO'D under reflection in BC. Name the transformation that maps AOD directly onto A"O"D".

10 Begin as with Question 9. Draw the image $A_2O_2D_2$ of AOD under reflection in BC. Draw the image $A_3O_3D_3$ of $A_2O_2D_2$ under reflection in AD. Name the transformation that maps AOD directly onto $A_3O_3D_3$.

11 Draw a rectangle as in Question 9. Draw any simple figure F, close to AB and just outside the rectangle. If R denotes reflection in AB and S denotes reflection in CD, draw $R(F)$ and $SR(F)$. Name the transformation that maps F directly onto $SR(F)$.
Draw $S(F)$ and $RS(F)$, and name the transformation that maps F directly onto $RS(F)$.

12 Draw a square WXYZ, with each side 3 cm long. Draw the triangle PXY, outside the square, with PX=1 cm and PXY=90°.
Draw $R(PXY)$, where R denotes a rotation of $-90°$ about X.
Draw $SR(PXY)$, where S denotes a rotation of 90° about Z. Describe the single transformation that maps PXY onto $SR(PXY)$.
Repeat the question but with S performed first and R second.

Vectors

Any quantity which has magnitude and direction can be represented by a straight line, called a **vector**, which has the same direction as the quantity, and whose length represents the magnitude on a suitable scale. Such a quantity is called a **vector quantity**: examples of vector quantities are **velocity** and **force**. A vector is always drawn with an arrow to show its direction.

This vector:

might represent a velocity of 50 km/h due eastward, on a scale of 1 cm to 10 km/h, or it might represent a force of 10 N, applied due eastward, on a scale of 1 cm to 2 N.

When a named line is to be regarded as a vector, this is shown by drawing an arrow above, thus $\overrightarrow{AB}$, or by printing in bold type, thus **AB**. Vectors are sometimes named by single letters, also printed in bold type.
In handwritten work, bold type is replaced by using a wavy underline, thus a̰

In Figure 8.4 ABCD is a rhombus, so it is correct to write AB=BC, since the lengths of AB and BC are equal, but it would be wrong to write **AB**=**BC** or $\overrightarrow{AB}=\overrightarrow{BC}$, because **AB** and **BC** are not equal **vectors**, as their directions are

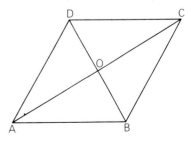

Figure 8.4

different. However it is correct to write **AB = DC**, since **AB** and **DC** are in the same direction, as well as being equal in length.

Sign of a vector In the same figure **AB** and **CD** are equal in length but in exactly opposite directions, so we write **AB = – CD**. We might also write **AB = – BA**.

Translations and vectors Since a translation has magnitude (distance) and direction, it can be completely represented by a vector.

Exercise 8.2

1 On a suitable scale draw vectors to represent

   a a displacement of 5 m northward
   b a velocity of 20 km/h westward
   c a force of 8 N acting southward
   d a translation of 20 cm eastward
   e a wind from the south-west with a speed of 60 knots

2 In Figure 8.5, state what is represented by **OB** if **OA** represents

   a a displacement of 2 m northward
   b a velocity of 200 km/h northward
   c a force of 10 N vertically upward
   d a south wind with a speed of 20 km/h
   e a translation of 20 cm parallel to the long sides of the paper

Figure 8.5

3 In Figure 8.3 name

   a 4 vectors equal to **AH**   **d** 4 vectors equal to **– AQ**
   b 4 vectors equal to **WO**   **e** 4 vectors equal to **– GO**
   c 4 vectors equal to **CR**

4 In Figure 8.3 name the member of each of the following sets of three vectors which is not equal to the other two members in that set.

   a AL, LW, MT   **c** RY, RU, UR   **e** BU, DY, EX
   b CI, LF, XR   **d** BL, MC, DN   **f** ES, PG, SJ

Addition of vectors

In Figure 8.6, the vector **AB** corresponds to a translation from F to

F', and the vector **BC** to a translation from F' to F''. The combined effect of the two translations is a translation from F to F'', and the vector that corresponds to this is **AC**. We therefore write **AB** + **BC** = **AC**, and can add all vectors in this way.

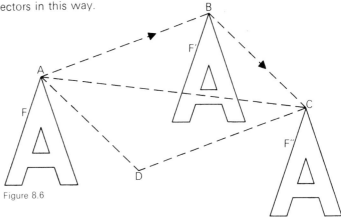

Figure 8.6

Looking at the parallelogram ABCD, we see that **AD** + **DC** = **AC**: since **AD** = **BC** and **DC** = **AB**, it follows that **BC** + **AB** = **AC**. This shows that in vector addition, as in ordinary addition of numbers, the *order* of the things being added does not matter. (This can be expressed by saying that addition of vectors, like addition of numbers, is *commutative*.)

Example 2

Figure 8.7 is a parallelogram. Name vectors equivalent to

a **AO** + **OB**   c **DA** + **OC**
b **OA** + **DC**

and write down three pairs of vectors such that the sum of each pair is **AB**.

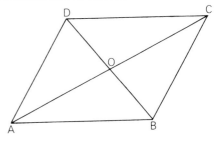

Figure 8.7

Answer
a **AO** + **OB** = **AB**
b **OA** + **DC** = **OA** + **AB** (since **DC** = **AB**) = **OB**
c **DA** + **OC** = **CB** + **OC** (since **DA** = **CB**) = **OC** + **CB** = **OB**
Three such pairs are, **AO** + **OB**, **AD** + **DB** and **AC** + **CB**.

Subtraction of vectors

Just as 8 − 3 is the same as 8 + (−3), so we take **AO** − **OB** (in Figure 8.7) as being the same as **AO** + (−**OB**), that is, as **AO** + **BO**, and since **BO** = **OD**, we have

$$\mathbf{AO} - \mathbf{OB} = \mathbf{AO} + \mathbf{OD} = \mathbf{AD}$$

In general, then, to **subtract** a vector, **add** the vector which has the same magnitude as the one which is being subtracted, but is in the opposite direction.

Example 3 In Figure 8.7, name vectors equivalent to

a **AO − OD**   b **AB − CB**   c **AO − OA**

and write down three pairs of vectors such that the difference of each pair is **BC**.

Answer

a **AO − OD = AO + DO**
            = AO + OB (since **DO = OB**)
            = AB
b **AB − CB = AB + BC = AC**
c **AO − OA = AO + AO**
            = AO + OC (since **AO = OC**)
            = AC

Three such pairs are **BO − CO**, **BA − CA** and **BD − CD**.

Multiplication of a vector by a number

Just as it is more convenient to write $3a$ than to write $a+a+a$, so it is more convenient to write $3\mathbf{AB}$ than **AB + AB + AB**. In Figure 8.7 **AC = AO + OC = AO + AO = 2AO**.

Exercise 8.3

1 In Figure 8.8 name single vectors equivalent to
   a **AC + CL**
   b **BG + GM**
   c **AK + FI**
   d **PG + CE**
   e **AK + FI**
   f **AP + OG**
   g **DO + NA**
   h **JO + NK**
   i **IL + HM**
   j **AB + AE + AK**

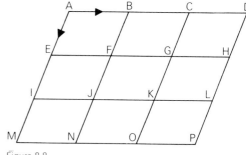

Figure 8.8

(Note that there are several possible correct answers to most of the parts of this question: this also applies to Questions 2, 3 and 4.)

CHAPTER 8 — TRANSLATION AND VECTORS

2 In Figure 8.8, name single vectors equivalent to

    a AG−GJ   d BL−GD   g AE−GO   j DH−BM
    b NB−BC   e AO+KN   h PK−LO
    c EO−JO   f MP−MN   i MC−JI

3 In Figure 8.8, name single vectors equivalent to

    a 2AB   c 3EJ   e −3NO   g $\frac{1}{3}$MA
    b 3CG   d −2LO   f $\frac{1}{2}$MG

4 In Figure 8.8, name single vectors equivalent to

    a 2AB+AJ   c 3GK+2CD   e 3CD−3DH
    b MP+2NI   d MP−2KP

5 **WX** and **YZ** are vectors such that **WX**=2**YZ**. What can be said about

    a the directions, and **b** the lengths of **WX** and **YZ**?

6 **p** and **q** are vectors such that **p**=−**q**. What can be said about

    a the directions, and **b** the lengths of **p** and **q**?

7 **a** and **b** are vectors such that **a**+3**b**=0. What can be said about

    a the directions, and **b** the lengths of **a** and **b**?

8 Vector **x** corresponds to translation T, and vector **y** corresponds to translation U. What vectors correspond to translations

    a TU c T^2 e TUT g TU^2
    b UT d U^2 f T^2U h T^2U^2?

9 In Figure 8.8, if **AB**=**r** and **AE**=**s**, express each of the following vectors in terms of **r** or **s** or both **r** and **s**.

    a GH   d JF   g PD   j KD   m AP
    b JN   e IK   h JO   k BM   n PA
    c PO   f BN   i EK   l MC

10 In Figure 8.9, **OA**=**AP**=**x**. **OB**=**BQ**=**y**. Express the following vectors in terms of **x** or **y** or both **x** and **y**.

    a AO   c AB   e PB
    b PO   d AQ   f PQ

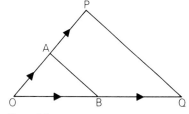

Figure 8.9

Write down two statements about the line segments AB and PQ which are implied by your answers to **c** and **f**.

11 In Figure 8.10, **OX**=**u**, **OZ**=**v** and OXYZ is a parallelogram. Express the following vectors in terms of **u** or **v** or both **u** and **v**.

  a YZ
  b XY
  c OY
  d OP, where P is the mid-point of OY
  e XZ
  f XQ, where Q is the mid-point of XZ
  g OQ

Figure 8.10

What property of the parallelogram is proved by your answers to **d** and **g**?

12 Use Figure 8.10. Assume that XZ and OY have the same mid-point (to be called P), but do not assume that OXYZ is a parallelogram. Take **XP** = **a**, **OP** = **b**. Express the following vectors in terms of **a** or **b** or both **a** and **b**.

  a XO   b PZ   c PY   d YZ   e XY   f OZ

How do your results prove that OXYZ is a parallelogram?

13 In Figure 8.11, **OX**=**XY**=**YB**=**p**, **OC**=**AB**=**q**. Express the following vectors in terms of **p** and **q**.

  a BC   c AY
  b OA   d CX

How do your results prove that triangles ABY and COX are congruent? Describe the transformation that maps one of them onto the other. Prove in a similar way that triangles AOY and CBX are congruent.

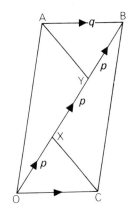

Figure 8.11

Column vectors

If coordinates are being used, any vector in the coordinate plane can be expressed as the sum of a vector in the x direction and one in the y direction: these are called the x and y **components** of the vector. In the diagram, **AP** and **PB** are the x and y components of **AB**. These components give a useful way of describing the vector, and can be formed into a column matrix thus $\begin{pmatrix} 3 \\ 4 \end{pmatrix}$. This is often called a *column vector* and this name is so widespread that it will be used here, although strictly speaking $\begin{pmatrix} 3 \\ 4 \end{pmatrix}$ is not a vector but a matrix describing a vector. It is convenient and customary to write, for example, **AB** $= \begin{pmatrix} 3 \\ 4 \end{pmatrix}$

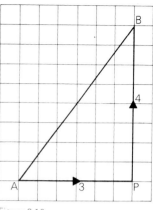

Figure 8.12

Length of a vector If the x and y components of a vector are known, its length can easily be calculated by using Pythagoras' theorem: in Figure 8.12, $AB^2 = AP^2 + BP^2 = 3^2 + 4^2 = 25$, so $AB = 5$. The length of a vector is sometimes called its *modulus* and is denoted by vertical lines, for example $|\mathbf{AB}| = 5$, $|\mathbf{p}| = Z$.

Example 4 The coordinates of A, B and C are respectively (1, 2), (9, 8) and (−3, 3). Write as column vectors **AB**, **BA**, **BC** and **CA**.

If **AD** $= \begin{pmatrix} 3 \\ 5 \end{pmatrix}$, find the coordinates of D. If **BE** $= \begin{pmatrix} -2 \\ -10 \end{pmatrix}$, find the coordinates of E. Find the lengths of AB and BC.

Answer
The x component of **AB** is $9 - 1 = 8$.
The y component of **AB** is $8 - 2 = 6$.
So **AB** $= \begin{pmatrix} 8 \\ 6 \end{pmatrix}$. In the same way, **BA** $= \begin{pmatrix} 1-9 \\ 2-8 \end{pmatrix} = \begin{pmatrix} -8 \\ -6 \end{pmatrix}$

BC $= \begin{pmatrix} -3-9 \\ 3-8 \end{pmatrix} = \begin{pmatrix} -12 \\ -5 \end{pmatrix}$ and **CA** $= \begin{pmatrix} 1--3 \\ 2-3 \end{pmatrix} = \begin{pmatrix} 4 \\ -1 \end{pmatrix}$

Since A is (1, 2) and **AD** $= \begin{pmatrix} 3 \\ 5 \end{pmatrix}$, the coordinates of D are $1+3$ and $2+5$, so D is (4, 7).

In the same way, the coordinates of E are $9 + -2$ and $8 + -10$, so E is (7, −2).

The components of **AB** are 8 and 6, so $AB^2 = 8^2 + 6^2$, giving $AB = 10$.

The components of **BC** are −12 and −5, so $BC^2 = (-12)^2 + (-5)^2$, giving $BC = 13$.

Exercise 8.4

1. The coordinates of P, Q and R are respectively (3, 1), (6, 5) and (−1, −2). Write as column vectors **PQ**, **QR** and **RP**, and find the lengths of PQ and RP.

2. The coordinates of D, E and F are respectively (4, 5), (−8, 10) and (−1, −7). Write as column vectors **DE**, **EF** and **FD**, and show that DEF is an isosceles triangle.

3. The coordinates of X, Y and Z are respectively (1, 2), (4, 7) and (6, −1). Write as column vectors **XY**, **YZ** and **ZX**. Find the lengths of all three vectors, and use the converse of Pythagoras' theorem to show that XYZ is a right-angled triangle.

4. Find the images of P, Q and R (as in Question 1) under a translation corresponding to the vector $\begin{pmatrix} 3 \\ -5 \end{pmatrix}$

5. T is the translation corresponding to the vector $\begin{pmatrix} 2 \\ -3 \end{pmatrix}$. Find the images of D, E and F (as in Question 2) under

   a T b T^2

6. U and V are the translations corresponding to $\begin{pmatrix} 7 \\ 0 \end{pmatrix}$ and $\begin{pmatrix} -4 \\ 3 \end{pmatrix}$ respectively. Find the images of X, Y and Z (as in Question 3) under

   a U b V c UV

7. PQRS is a parallelogram (P, Q and R as in Questions 1 and 4). Write down **PS** as a column vector and hence find the coordinates of S.

8. G is the fourth vertex of a parallelogram whose other vertices are D, E and F (as in Questions 2 and 5), not necessarily in that order. Find the coordinates of three possible positions of G.

9. W is a point such that **XW** = **YX** (X, Y, Z as in Questions 3 and 6). Find the coordinates of W. Find also the coordinates of V if WVYZ is a square.

10. O is (0, 0), **OA** = $\begin{pmatrix} 2 \\ 0 \end{pmatrix}$, **AB** = $\begin{pmatrix} 2 \\ -1 \end{pmatrix}$, **BC** = $\begin{pmatrix} 1 \\ -4 \end{pmatrix}$. Find the coordinates of A, B and C, and the vector **CO**.

11. H is (4, −1) and K is (−2, 3). Find the coordinates of

    a L if K is the mid-point of HL
    b M if H is the mid-point of MK
    c N if L is the mid-point of MN

12 P is the point with coordinates (x, y), $\mathbf{PQ} = \begin{pmatrix} a \\ b \end{pmatrix}$ and $\mathbf{PR} = \begin{pmatrix} -b \\ a \end{pmatrix}$.

Write down expressions for the coordinates of Q and R, and show that the lengths of PQ and PR are equal.

Express **QR** as a column vector, and find an expression for its length. Hence show that angle QPR is a right angle.

Addition, subtraction and multiplication by a number

It is clear from Figure 8.13 that the sum of $\begin{pmatrix} a \\ b \end{pmatrix}$ and $\begin{pmatrix} c \\ d \end{pmatrix}$ is $\begin{pmatrix} a+c \\ b+d \end{pmatrix}$, that is, the rule for adding vectors corresponds to the rule for adding matrices. The same applies to subtraction and multiplication by a number.

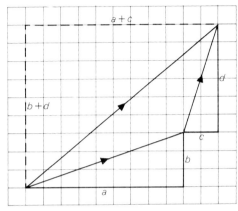

Figure 8.13

Example 5   If $\mathbf{a} = \begin{pmatrix} 1 \\ 2 \end{pmatrix}$, $\mathbf{b} = \begin{pmatrix} -3 \\ 4 \end{pmatrix}$ find column vectors for $\mathbf{a} + \mathbf{b}$, $\mathbf{b} - \mathbf{a}$, $\mathbf{a} - \mathbf{b}$, $2\mathbf{a}$, $3\mathbf{b}$ and $3\mathbf{a} - 4\mathbf{b}$.

Answer

$$\mathbf{a} + \mathbf{b} = \begin{pmatrix} 1 + -3 \\ 2 + 4 \end{pmatrix} = \begin{pmatrix} -2 \\ 6 \end{pmatrix}$$

$$\mathbf{a} - \mathbf{b} = \begin{pmatrix} 1 - -3 \\ 2 - 4 \end{pmatrix} = \begin{pmatrix} 4 \\ -2 \end{pmatrix} \quad \mathbf{b} - \mathbf{a} = \begin{pmatrix} -3 - 1 \\ 4 - 2 \end{pmatrix} = \begin{pmatrix} -4 \\ 2 \end{pmatrix}$$

$$2\mathbf{a} = 2 \begin{pmatrix} 1 \\ 2 \end{pmatrix} = \begin{pmatrix} 2 \\ 4 \end{pmatrix}, \quad 3\mathbf{b} = 3 \begin{pmatrix} -3 \\ 4 \end{pmatrix} = \begin{pmatrix} -9 \\ 12 \end{pmatrix}$$

$$3\mathbf{a} - 4\mathbf{b} = 3 \begin{pmatrix} 1 \\ 2 \end{pmatrix} - 4 \begin{pmatrix} -3 \\ 4 \end{pmatrix} = \begin{pmatrix} 3 \\ 6 \end{pmatrix} - \begin{pmatrix} -12 \\ 16 \end{pmatrix} = \begin{pmatrix} 15 \\ -10 \end{pmatrix}$$

Example 6   If **a** and **b** have the same meanings as in Example 5, find two numbers, p and q, such that $p\mathbf{a} + q\mathbf{b} = \begin{pmatrix} -1 \\ 18 \end{pmatrix}$.

Answer

Since $p \begin{pmatrix} 1 \\ 2 \end{pmatrix} + q \begin{pmatrix} -3 \\ 4 \end{pmatrix} = \begin{pmatrix} -1 \\ 18 \end{pmatrix}$, we can write $p - 3q = -1$
$2p + 4q = 18$.

These equations can be solved simultaneously in the usual way, giving $p = 5$, $q = 2$.

Exercise 8.5

1. If $u = \begin{pmatrix} 2 \\ -3 \end{pmatrix}$ and $v = \begin{pmatrix} -1 \\ 4 \end{pmatrix}$, find column vectors for

   a $u + v$
   b $u - v$
   c $v - u$
   d $4u$
   e $-3v$
   f $2u + 5v$
   g $3u - 2v$

2. If $p = \begin{pmatrix} -5 \\ 0 \end{pmatrix}$ and $q = \begin{pmatrix} 6 \\ -2 \end{pmatrix}$, find column vectors for

   a $p + q$
   b $p - q$
   c $q - p$
   d $-2p$
   e $5q$
   f $-3p - 2q$
   g $2p - \tfrac{1}{2}q$

3. if $c = \begin{pmatrix} -2 \\ -3 \end{pmatrix}$ and $d = \begin{pmatrix} 0 \\ 4 \end{pmatrix}$, find column vectors for

   a $c + d$
   b $c - d$
   c $d - c$
   d $3c + 4d$
   e $4c - 3d$
   f $\tfrac{1}{3}c + \tfrac{1}{2}d$
   g $\tfrac{1}{4}d - 3c$

4. If u and v have the same meanings as in Question 1, solve the following equations (in each case r is the vector to be found).

   a $2r = u$
   b $r + u = v$
   c $r - 2v = 3u$
   d $2r + 2v = u$

5. If p and q have the same meanings as in Question 2, solve the following equations (in each case r is the vector to be found).

   a $r + 2p = q$
   b $q - 2r = p$
   c $2r + 3p = -q$
   d $3q + 2r = -4p$

6. If c and d have the same meanings as in Question 3, find

   a numbers h and k such that $hc + kd = \begin{pmatrix} 4 \\ 2 \end{pmatrix}$

   b numbers m and n such that $mc + nd = \begin{pmatrix} -6 \\ -5 \end{pmatrix}$

7. If $r = \begin{pmatrix} 3 \\ 1 \end{pmatrix}$ and $s = \begin{pmatrix} -2 \\ 4 \end{pmatrix}$, find

   a numbers p and q such that $pr + qs = \begin{pmatrix} 7 \\ 7 \end{pmatrix}$

   b numbers t and u such that $tr + us = \begin{pmatrix} 8 \\ 5 \end{pmatrix}$

8. $AB = \begin{pmatrix} 3 \\ 2 \end{pmatrix}$, and $AX = -2AB$; $AC = \begin{pmatrix} 4 \\ -3 \end{pmatrix}$ and $AY = -2AC$. Find column vectors for **BC** and **XY**. What do these results show, concerning the lines BC and XY?

9. Repeat Question 8, but with $AB = \begin{pmatrix} 1 \\ 5 \end{pmatrix}$ and $AC = \begin{pmatrix} -2 \\ 3 \end{pmatrix}$.

10. The coordinates of P and Q are respectively (3, 4) and (1, −2). Find column vectors for **PQ** and $\tfrac{1}{2}$**PQ**. Hence find the coordinates of the midpoint of PQ.

CHAPTER 8 — TRANSLATION AND VECTORS

11 Repeat Question 10, but take the coordinates of P and Q as (4, 5) and (−2, 1) respectively. Can you see any connection between the coordinates of the mid-point of PQ and those of P and Q?

12 Repeat Question 10, but take the coordinates of P and Q as (a, b) and (c, d) respectively. Simplify your results as much as possible.

13 The vertices of a quadrilateral are (0, 0), (2, 4), (−2, 8) and (−4, 6) respectively. Use the results of Questions 10, 11 and 12 to find the coordinates of the mid-points of the sides of the quadrilateral: call these, in order, W, X, Y and Z. Find column vectors for **WX** and **ZY**. What kind of quadrilateral is WXYZ?

14 Repeat Question 13 but taking the vertices of the quadrilateral as any four points of your own choosing.

15 $OP = \begin{pmatrix} -1 \\ 5 \end{pmatrix}$, $OQ = \begin{pmatrix} 8 \\ 2 \end{pmatrix}$ and OPRQ is a parallelogram: find column vectors for **OR** and **PQ**.

S is the mid-point of PR, and T is a point such that $OT = \frac{2}{3}OS$. Find column vectors for **PS**, **OS**, **OT** and **PT**. What do your results prove about the points P, T and Q?

Exercise 8.6 Reflection, rotation and translation

1 Figure 8.14 shows the triangles A, B, C and D. Describe as fully as possible transformations that map

 a A onto B,
 b A onto C,
 c A onto D,
 d B onto C (two possible transformations),
 e B onto D,
 f C onto D.

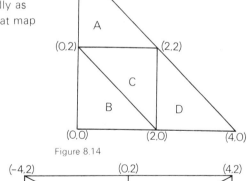

Figure 8.14

2 Figure 8.15 shows a pattern of eight right-angled triangles, lettered A to H. T, U, V, W and X are transformations such that $T(A) = B$, $U(A) = D$, $V(A) = E$, $W(A) = F$, and $X(A) = H$.

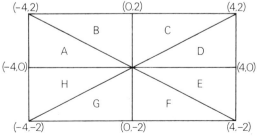

Figure 8.15

Describe fully each of the transformations *T*, *U*, *V*, *W* and *X*.
Name the image of A under *UT*, and find a pair of transformations that maps A onto G (these transformations to be chosen from *T*, *U*, *V*, *W* and *X*).

3 With the figure and notation of Question 2, name

    a *U*(H)   **c** *V*(C)   **e** *UV*(D)
    b *W*(B)   **d** *X*(F)   **f** *UVX*(G)

4 With Figure 8.15, describe as fully as possible single transformations that map

    a C onto H   **b** E onto F   **c** G onto D   **d** H onto G

5 Describe *five* transformations that map the left-hand square onto the right-hand one in Figure 8.16 (describe a translation by naming the corresponding vector), and name the image of A in each case.

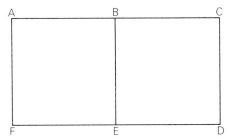

Figure 8.16

6 *T* and *U* are translations, *R* and *S* are rotations, *M* and *N* are reflections. Name the possible kind or kinds of transformations

    a that *TU* could be,   **c** that *TR* could be,
    b that *RS* could be,   **d** that *MN* could be.

Could *TM* be a translation or a rotation or a reflection? Could *RM*? (Assume that none of the composite transformations returns a figure to its original position.)

7 Which of the composite transformations mentioned in Question 6 *could* return a figure to its original position? In each case where it is possible, describe the conditions under which it would happen.

Chapter 9
Inequalities

The student who has reached this chapter will certainly be familiar with some method for solving simple linear equations – perhaps like this:

$$\begin{array}{ll} \text{To solve the equation} & 2x+3=9, \\ \text{Take 3 from both sides} & 2x=6 \\ \text{Divide both sides by 2} & x=3 \end{array}$$

However, in many aspects of life *inequality* is a much commoner state of affairs than equality (as is illustrated in the picture here). If all we know is that $2x+3$ is **not** equal to 9 (written $2x+3 \neq 9$), then all we can say about x is that x is **not** equal to 3 ($x \neq 3$): this is probably not very useful, but if we know whether $2x+3$ is **more** or **less** than 9, we can at least find a range (or set) of possible values for x. The work is the same as in solving the equation: if one side of the inequality is larger, it will remain larger even when 3 has been taken from **both** sides and when **both** sides

have been divided by 2. The working would be as follows (the symbol > means 'is more than').

$$2x+3>9$$
take 3 from both sides $\quad 2x>6$
divide both sides by 2 $\quad x>3$

So the inequality is satisfied by any value of x which is more than 3.

In solving an inequality, as in solving an equation, we can carry out the following processes:

1 Adding the same number to both sides
2 Subtracting the same number from both sides
3 Multiplying both sides by the same *positive* number
4 Dividing both sides by the same *positive* number

Note that in **3** and **4** a *positive* number is specified. This is an important difference between solving an inequality and solving an equation. If $-x = -3$, then $x=3$, but if $-x>-3$ then x is *less* than 3 as can easily be seen by substituting numbers for x:

$$-2>-3 \text{ but } 2<3$$
$$-4<-3 \text{ but } 4>3$$

We thus have the important rule:

If both sides of an inequality are multiplied or divided by a *negative* number, the inequality symbol must be reversed.

The following symbols are used:

> means 'is more than'
≥ means 'is more than or equal to'
< means 'is less than'
≤ means 'is less than or equal to'

Example 1   Solve the inequality $\quad \dfrac{x+1}{3} - \dfrac{x-1}{2} > x$

Answer
Multiply both sides by 6 $2(x+1) - 3(x-1) > 6x$,

Remove brackets $2x + 2 - 3x + 3 > 6x$

Collect terms $-x + 5 > 6x$

Take $6x$ from both sides, and take 5 from both sides,

$$-7x > -5,$$

Divide both sides by -7 *and reverse the inequality symbol*

$$x < \frac{5}{7}$$

CHAPTER 9 — INEQUALITIES

Example 2 Find the set of values of x for which $\quad 2x-5 \leqslant x-2 \leqslant \dfrac{3x}{2}$

Answer
Here there are two inequalities, which must be dealt with separately.

$$2x - 5 \leqslant x - 2$$

Add 5 to both sides $\qquad\qquad\qquad\qquad 2x \leqslant x + 3$

Take x from both sides $\qquad\qquad\qquad x \leqslant 3$

Also $\qquad\qquad\qquad\qquad\qquad\qquad x - 2 \leqslant \dfrac{3x}{2}$

Multiply by 2 $\qquad\qquad\qquad\qquad\quad 2x - 4 \leqslant 3x$

Take $2x$ from both sides $\qquad\qquad\quad -4 \leqslant x$

This is equivalent to $x \geqslant -4$ so both inequalities are satisfied when x has any value between (and including) -4 and 3, i.e. when $-4 \leqslant x \leqslant 3$.

Exercise 9.1

1 Solve these inequalities

    a $3x > 12$ **d** $\dfrac{x}{7} \leqslant 1$ **g** $x + 2\tfrac{1}{2} \geqslant 2\tfrac{1}{4}$

    b $x - 4 < 5$ **e** $-3x > 9$ **h** $5 - x \leqslant 3$

    c $x + 5 \geqslant 2$ **f** $-2x < -8$ **i** $\dfrac{2x}{5} > \dfrac{7}{10}$

2 Solve these inequalities.

    a $3x - 2 > 7$ **d** $\dfrac{x}{6} + 3 > -2$ **g** $4 - 3x < -5$

    b $2x + 5 < 1$ **e** $10 - 2x \geqslant 1$ **h** $\dfrac{2x+3}{5} > \tfrac{1}{2}$

    c $\dfrac{x+4}{3} \geqslant 2$ **f** $-3x - 7 \leqslant -5$

3 Solve these inequalities.

    a $2x + 3 > x + 7$ **d** $7 - 2x < 9 - 5x$ **f** $10 - 3x \leqslant 2x + 5$
    b $x - 5 \leqslant 3x + 4$ **e** $4x + 7 \geqslant 1 - 4x$ **g** $-3 - 4x > 7x + 8$
    c $3x - 2 \geqslant 6 - x$

4 Solve these inequalities.

a $3(x+5) < 7(x-7)$ **d** $6(7-2x) > 7(6-2x)$ **f** $5(8+3x) \geqslant -4(7-3x)$
b $2(x-9) \leqslant 5(2-x)$ **e** $3(3x+1) < 7-4x$ **g** $-2(9-3x) \leqslant 12x$
c $4(2x+1) \geqslant -12x$

5 Solve these inequalities.

a $\frac{1}{2}x+1 < \frac{1}{4}x-2$ **d** $\frac{2}{3}(1-5x) \leqslant \frac{3}{4}(2-3x)$ **f** $\frac{x}{5}+\frac{2x-5}{3} < 17-x$

b $\frac{1}{2}(x-4) \geqslant \frac{1}{3}(3-x)$ **e** $\frac{2x-1}{3} > \frac{3x-4}{4}$ **g** $\frac{4-x}{3}-\frac{3-x}{4} \geqslant \frac{1-x}{6}$

c $\frac{x}{5}+\frac{x+1}{3} < 3$

6 Find the ranges of values of x which satisfy each of the following pairs of inequalities. Give your answers in the form $a < x < b$ or $a \leqslant x \leqslant b$, where a and b are the numbers you have to find.

a $2x+1 > x > 3x-2$ **c** $x+1 \geqslant 5-x \geqslant 3x-7$
b $3-x \geqslant 2x \geqslant -10-3x$ **d** $\frac{2}{3}x-\frac{3}{4} < \frac{1}{2}x-\frac{1}{2} < \frac{3}{4}x-\frac{2}{3}$

Solution sets

The solution of an inequality consists of a set of numbers, and can be expressed in set notation. For example, the solution of Example 2 (page 00) can be written $\{x: -4 < x < 3\}$, read as 'the set of numbers x such that x lies between -4 and 3'.

If the universal set is {integers} or some other restricted set of numbers, it may be possible to give the solution set in list form. For example, if $\mathscr{E}$ = {integers} and $A = \{x: 1 \leqslant x \leqslant 5\}$, then $A = \{1, 2, 3, 4, 5\}$.

Number lines

Sets of numbers, whether they are the solution sets of inequalities or not, can be represented on number lines, which can be drawn horizontally or vertically. The best way to understand this is to study an example: the solution set of Example 2 can be represented as in Figure 9.1.

Figure 9.1

The thick line indicates the set: the 'hollow' white dots at its ends indicate that the numbers -4 and 3 do not belong to the set. If the end numbers *do* belong to the set, (for example, if the set were x: $-4 \leqslant x \leqslant 3$) this is indicated by the use of solid black dots as shown in Figure 9.2.

CHAPTER 9 — INEQUALITIES

Figure 9.2

Example 3 Find the solution set of the pair of inequalities

$3x+1 \geqslant 7 > 5x-13$

and represent the solution on a number line.
If $\mathscr{E}=\{\text{integers}\}$ give the solution set in list form.

Answer
1   $3x+1 \geqslant 7$ gives $x \geqslant 2$
2   $7 > 5x-13$ gives $x < 4$
The solution set is $x: 2 \leqslant x < 4$
On the number line this is shown as in Figure 9.3.

Figure 9.3

If $\mathscr{E}=\{\text{integers}\}$ the solution set is $\{2, 3\}$
Note: '$\mathscr{E}=$integers' does not apply when the solution is shown on the number line.

Example 4 If $x \in \{x: 4 < x < 7\}$ and $y \in \{y: 1 < y < 3\}$, find the set of possible values

a of $x+y$ **b** of $x-y$

Answer
$x+y$ takes its largest value when x and y take their largest values, and similarly with the smallest values. So $5 < x+y < 10$.

$x-y$ takes its largest value when x takes its largest and y its smallest value, so the largest value of $x-y$ is 6; similarly its smallest value is 1 (when $x=4$ and $y=3$.) So $1 < x-y < 6$.

Exercise 9.2

1   Represent each of the following sets on a number line:

   a $\{x: -3 < x < 2\}$ **c** $\{x: 3 \geqslant x > -4\}$
   b $\{x: 7 \geqslant x \geqslant 0\}$ **d** $\{x: -2 > x \geqslant -7\}$

2   Name the sets represented on each of the number lines in Figure 9.4.

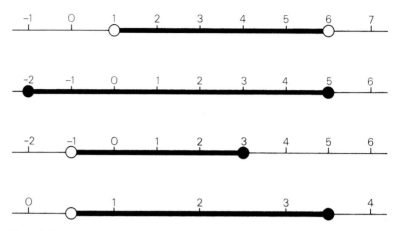

Figure 9.4

3 If $\mathscr{E}=\{$positive integers$\}$, give in list form the solution sets of

  a $3x+1 \leqslant 15$ **d** $10-2x>3>10-4x$
  b $15-2x>1$ **e** $10-x>2x+5>4x+2$
  c $2x+1<5x<3x+7$

4 For each of the following pairs of sets, A and B, write '$A \subset B$' or '$B \subset A$' or '$A \not\subset B$ and $B \not\subset A$', according to which statement is true.

  a $A=\{x: -2<x<2\}$, $B=\{x: -2 \leqslant x \leqslant 2\}$
  b $A=\{x: -2 \leqslant x<2\}$, $B=\{x: -2<x \leqslant 2\}$
  c $A=\{x: -2 \leqslant x \leqslant 2\}$, $B=\{-2, -1, 0, 1, 2\}$
  d $A=\{x: -2<x<2\}$, $B=\{-2, -1, 0, 1, 2\}$
  e $A=\{x: -2<x<2\}$, $B=\{x: 0<x<2\}$

5 Find, and represent on a number line, the solution set of each of these inequalities.

  a $9-2x<6+x<14-x$ **c** $\tfrac{1}{2}x+1 \geqslant 7-x>x-9$
  b $x+2 \leqslant 3x \leqslant x+8$ **d** $x^2 \leqslant 9$

6 If $x \in \{x: 1<x<5\}$ and $y \in \{y: 10<y<15\}$ find the sets of possible values of

  a $x+y$ **b** $y-x$ **c** xy **d** $\dfrac{y}{x}$ **e** $\dfrac{x}{y}$

7 If $a \in \{a: -3 \leqslant a \leqslant 3\}$, and $b \in \{b: -1 \leqslant b \leqslant 2\}$ find the sets of possible values of

  a $a+b$ **b** $a-b$ **c** ab **d** a^2 **e** a^2-b^2

CHAPTER 9 — INEQUALITIES

8 If $x+y>7$, and $x-y>1$
   a find 3 possible pairs of integral values of x and y
   b prove that $x>4$
   c find the set of possible values of y if $x<10$

9 If $x>y>0$, and $2x+y<8$
   a find 3 possible pairs of integral values of x and y
   b prove that $x<4$
   c find the set of possible values of x, and the set of possible values of y.

10 If $\mathscr{E}=\{$positive integers, not including 0$\}$, find the set of pairs of values of x and y that satisfy $x+y\leqslant 4$ and $y>x$.

11 If $\mathscr{E}=\{$positive integers, not including 0$\}$, find the set of pairs of values of x and y that satisfy $y>2x$ and $y-x\leqslant 3$.

12 The length and breadth of a rectangle are integral numbers of centimetres: its area is more than 16 cm² and its perimeter is less than 20 cm. Find the set of possible pairs of dimensions (lengths and breadths) of the rectangle.

13 'At least six of my class were away to-day', said Billy, 'and that's nearly a quarter of the class'. Given that no class in Billy's school has more than thirty children, find the set of possible values

   a of children absent,   **b** of children present.

14 With a tenpenny piece you cannot buy three Sweetipops, but if you buy ten you get some change from a 50p piece. Find the set of possible prices for a Sweetipop.

15 Find the sets of pairs of positive integral non-zero values of x and y,
   a that satisfy $x+2y<5$ **c** that satisfy $7<x+2y<8$
   b that satisfy $5<x+2y<7$

16 Find the set of values of x for which the inequality $x^2<x$ is satisfied.

17 Find which of the following statements are true. If any statement is untrue, make up an example to show that it is untrue.
   a If $x>3$, then $x^2>9$ **c** If $x^2>9$, then $x>3$
   b If $x<3$, then $x^2<9$ **d** If $x^2<9$, then $x<3$

Degrees of accuracy

When the value of a number is given to a certain degree of accuracy, this means that the value is stated to belong to a certain set of numbers. For example, if it is stated that the length of a rectangle is 15 cm to the nearest centimetre, this means that $14.5 \leqslant l < 15.5$, where l is te length in centimetres. Note that the set includes 14.5 but not 15.5; if the value were 15.5 it would be given as 16 to the nearest centimetre.

A number that has been calculated from other numbers which are correct to specified degrees of accuracy is of course itself correct only to a certain degree of accuracy; the set of numbers to which it must belong can be calculated.

Example 5   The length and breadth of a rectangle are given as 15 cm and 11 cm to the nearest centimetre. Find the set of possible values of its area, and find to how many significant figures its area can be given.

Answer
If l, b and A are respectively the length and breadth in centimetres and the area in square centimetres, then

$$14.5 \leqslant l < 15.5$$
$$10.5 \leqslant b < 11.5$$
so $14.5 \times 10.5 \leqslant A < 15.5 \times 11.5$
i.e. $152.25 \leqslant A < 178.25$

A can be given with certainty to only one significant figure. Note that although l and b are given to the nearest centimetre and to two significant figures, A cannot be given to the nearest square centimetre or even to the nearest 10 cm², nor to two significant figures.

Example 6   A pile of sheets of paper is measured as being 8.4 cm thick, to the nearest millimetre, and the number of sheets in the pile is between 110 and 120, both numbers inclusive. Find the set of possible values of the thickness of a sheet.

Answer
The largest possible value is given by taking the largest total thickness with the *smallest* number of sheets, and so is just under $8.45 \div 110$, i.e. 0.0768 cm, or 0.768 mm. The smallest possible value is $8.35 \div 120$ cm, i.e. 0.0696 cm or 0.696 mm.

So $0.696 \leqslant t < 0.768$, where t is the thickness in millimetres.

Exercise 9.3

1   If $a = 3$ and $b = 4$, both correct to one significant figure, find the set of possible values of

    a $a + b$ **b** $b - a$ **c** ab **d** $\dfrac{b}{a}$

CHAPTER 9 — INEQUALITIES

2 The length and breadth of a rectangle are measured as 37 cm and 23 cm, correct to the nearest centimetre. Find the set of possible values of the perimeter.

3 A girl says it takes her 11 minutes to walk to school, a distance of $\tfrac{3}{4}$ mile. If the time may be wrong by up to 1 minute either way, and the distance is correct only to the nearest quarter-mile, find the set of possible values of her average speed.

4 A number (n) of grains of rice is found to weigh 10 g to the nearest gram. Given that $480 < n < 500$, find the set of possible values of the average weight of one grain. Give your answers to two significant figures.

5 A guide-book gives the following distances.

> Reading to Newbury   15 miles
> Newbury to Marlborough   19 miles
> Marlborough to Calne   13 miles
> Calne to Chippenham   6 miles

Assuming that all these distances are given to the nearest mile, find the set of possible values of the distance from Reading to Chippenham by this route (according to the information given).

6 Three angles of a quadrilateral are measured to the nearest degree and found to be 106°, 84° and 77°. Find the set of possible values of the fourth angle.

Tables of squares and square roots are needed for the next two questions.

7 The triangle ABC is right-angled at A. AB = 4.3 cm and AC = 2.8 cm, correct to two significant figures. Use square and square root tables to find the set of possible values of the length of BC.

8 The triangle XYZ is right-angled at X. YZ = 9.2 cm and XY = 5.3 cm, correct to two significant figures. Use square and square root tables to find the set of possible values of the length of XZ.

9 A class of children were asked to measure the radius of a circle and to calculate its circumference. Their estimates of the radius ranged from 2.8 cm to 3.0 cm. Some of them took π as 3.14, some took π as 3.142, and some took π as $3\tfrac{1}{7}$. Find the largest and smallest possible values of their results for the circumference, assuming that they carried out the calculations correctly.

Chapter 10
Enlargement and similarity

In the three transformations studied so far in this book, the image has always been congruent to (i.e. of the same size and shape as) the figure transformed. We now encounter a transformation in which the figure and its image are the same shape but of different sizes, like the statues in the picture (though of course the statues are three-dimensional and nearly all the work of this chapter concerns two-dimensional figures.)

CHAPTER 10 — ENLARGEMENT AND SIMILARITY

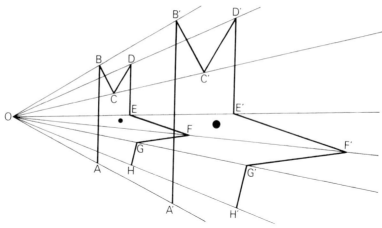

Figure 10.1

Draw a simple figure ABCDEFGH, perhaps like that shown above. Mark a point O outside the figure. Draw the lines OA, OB, OC etc. and produce them to points A', B', C' etc. so that OA'=2OA, OB'=2OB and so on. Join the points A'B'C'D' etc. to form a figure which is the image of ABCDEFGH under an *enlargement* with centre O and *scale factor* 2.

Check by measurement that

1 A'B'=2AB, B'C'=2BC and so on, for all the sides of the image figure. Check also a few of the 'diagonal' lengths, e.g. A'C', to see that a corresponding result applies to them.

2 every side of A'B'C'D'E'F'G'H' is parallel to the corresponding side of ABCDEFGH. Check a few of the 'diagonal' lines also.

3 angle A'B'C'=angle ABC, and every angle of the image figure is equal to the corresponding angle of the original figure.

If the image had been drawn with OA'=3OA, OB'=3OB and so on, the scale factor of the enlargement would have been 3: similarly an image can be drawn under an enlargement with any required scale factor

We can prove that if A'B'C'... is the image of ABC... under an enlargement with centre O and scale factor k, then A'B'=kAB, B'C'=kBC and so on, also that A'B', B'C' etc. are respectively parallel to AB, BC etc.

For **A'B'=OB'−OA'**=k**OB**−k**OA**= k(**OB**−**OA**)=k**AB**, which implies both the required results. The result that angle A'B'C'=angle ABC also follows at once, from the fact that the lines are parallel.

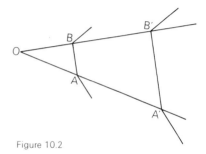

Figure 10.2

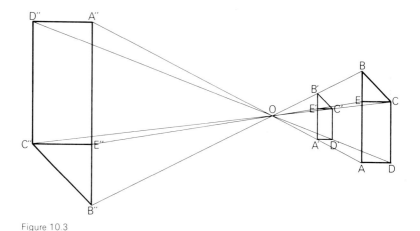

Figure 10.3

Fractional and negative scale factors

In Figure 10.3, $OA' = \frac{1}{2}OA$, $OB' = \frac{1}{2}OB$ and so on: A'B'C'... is the image of ABC... under an enlargement with scale factor $\frac{1}{2}$. It is, rather surprisingly, still called an enlargement, even though the image is smaller than the original figure.

A"B"C"... is the image of ABC... under an enlargement with a *negative* scale factor, namely -2. To draw this, the lines OA, OB etc. are drawn back through O, so that $OA" = 2AO$, $OB" = 2BO$, etc.

It will be seen that results **1**, **2** and **3** on page 87 still apply, even when the scale factor of the enlargement is fractional or negative.

Exercise 10.1

1 Draw a small irregular quadrilateral ABCD, and mark a point O outside it. Draw the images of ABCD under enlargements with centre O and the following scale factors:
   a 3   **b** 4   **c** $\frac{1}{2}$ **d** -2 **e** -3

2 Repeat Question 1, but with O inside the quadrilateral.

3 Repeat Question 1, but with A as the centre of enlargement.

4 Draw another small figure and draw its images under enlargements, both with scale factor 2, but with different centres, O and P. Describe the transformation that maps one of the two images onto the other.

CHAPTER 10 — ENLARGEMENT AND SIMILARITY

5 Figure X is mapped onto figure Y by an enlargement with centre O and scale factor 3. Describe the transformation that maps figure Y onto figure X.

Figure Y is mapped onto figure Z by an enlargement with centre O and scale factor -2. Describe the transformations that map figures

a X onto Z **b** Z onto Y **c** Z onto X

6 Plot the points A(0, 1), B(0, 2) and C(2, 1). Draw the image of ABC under E, an enlargement with centre (0, 0) and scale factor 3. Find the area of ABC and the area of E(ABC). What is the *area scale factor* of E, that is, the ratio of the area of the image under E to that of the original figure? Draw the image of ABC under F, an enlargement with centre (2, 0) and scale factor 3. What is the area scale factor of F? Describe a transformation that maps E(ABC) onto F(ABC).

7 Draw A, B, C and E(ABC) as in Question 6. Draw also G(ABC), where G is an enlargement with centre (0, 0) and scale factor -3. What is the area scale factor of G? Describe **a** an enlargement, and **b** a transformation, other than an enlargement, either of which would map E(ABC) onto G(ABC).

8 Plot the points P(3, 6), Q(6, 0) and R(-3, -3). Draw the image of PQR under H, an enlargement with centre (0, 0) and scale factor $\frac{1}{3}$. Find the areas of PQR and H(PQR), and the area scale factor of H.

Draw the image of PQR under K, an enlargement with centre (0, 0) and scale factor $-\frac{1}{2}$. Find the area scale factor of K.

Describe the transformations that map

a H(PQR) onto K(PQR), **b** K(PQR) onto H(PQR).

9 For every enlargement in this question, the centre is (2, -1). Find the scale factors of the enlargements that map

a (1, 1) onto (0, 3) **c** (-2, 1) onto (0, 0)
b (1, 0) onto (4, -3) **d** (0, -2) onto (5, $\frac{1}{2}$)

Find the image of (4, 3) under each of these enlargements.

Area scale factor

The student who has worked through the above examples, or most of them, will realise that the area scale factor of an enlargement is simply the square of the ordinary scale factor. (The ordinary scale factor is sometimes called the *linear* scale factor to distinguish it from the area scale factor and possibly other scale factors.) This is further illustrated in Figure 10.4.

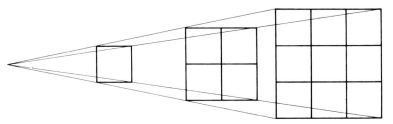

Figure 10.4

Finding the centre

If two figure ABC...A'B'C'... are such that A'B' is parallel to AB, B'C' is parallel to BC and so on, and also the lengths A'B', B'C' etc. are proportional to the lengths AB, BC etc., then each of the two figures is the image of the other under an enlargement. The centre of the enlargement is most easily found by joining corresponding pairs of points AA', BB' and so on, producing the lines if necessary until they meet at the centre of enlargement.

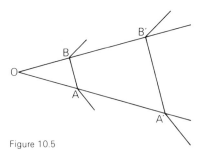

Figure 10.5

We can prove that the above statement is true. If $\dfrac{A'B'}{AB} = \dfrac{B'C'}{BC} = \ldots = k$, we can find a point O on A'A, produced if necessary, so that $A'O = kAO$. (The diagram illustrates the case when k is positive; if k is negative, O will lie between A and A'.)

Then **OB'** = **OA'** + **A'B'** = k**OA** + k**AB**
          = k(**OA** + **AB**) = k**OB**, and **OB'** = k**OB**, with O, B, B' in line. Similarly **OC'** = k**OC** and so on, and this is the definition of an enlargement.

CHAPTER 10 — ENLARGEMENT AND SIMILARITY

Example 1 The triangle whose vertices are A(1, 0), B(0, 2) and O(0, 0) is mapped onto the triangle whose vertices are C(0, 4), D(2, 0) and P(2, 4) by means of an enlargement. Find the centre and the scale factor of this enlargement, and also of the enlargement that maps triangle CDP onto triangle ABO.

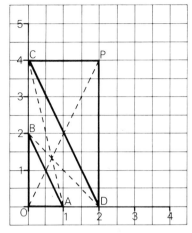

Figure 10.6

Answer
Looking at Figure 10.6, it is clear that O and P are corresponding points (since it is at these vertices that the triangles are right-angled); similarly A corresponds to C, and B to D. Join these points, as shown by the dotted lines in the figure; they meet at $(\frac{2}{3}, 1\frac{1}{3})$, which is therefore the centre of enlargement.

Each side of CDP is twice as long as the corresponding side of ABO (for example, DP=4, BO=2) so the scale factor is −2. It is negative because the points and their images, for example O and P, lie on opposite sides of the centre.

If CDP is mapped onto ABO, the centre is the same, but the scale factor is $-\frac{1}{2}$, since each side of ABO is *half* as long as the corresponding side of CDP.

Example 2

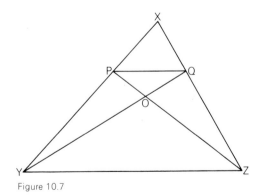

Figure 10.7

In Figure 10.7, XPQ is the image of triangle XYZ under an enlargement with centre X and scale factor $\frac{1}{3}$. Describe the transformation that maps POQ onto ZOY. If triangle POQ has area 1 unit, find the areas of triangles POY, YOZ, QOZ, XPQ and XYZ.

Answer
POQ is mapped onto ZOY by an enlargement with centre O, since O is mapped onto itself. Since PQ=⅓YZ, the scale factor must be −3.

This means OY=3OQ. OY and OQ can be regarded as the bases of triangles POY and POQ, which have the same height (i.e. the perpendicular distance of P from YQ), and so have areas proportional to their bases. Thus area POY=3 × area POQ=3 units.

The *area* scale factor of the enlargement that maps POQ onto ZOY is 9, so area ZOY=9 units.

Area QOZ=3 units, by the same kind of reasoning as for POY.

The *area* scale factor of the enlargement that maps XYZ onto XPQ is ⅑, so XPQ has ⅑ the area of XYZ, or ⅛ the area of quadrilateral PQZY. Area PQZY=POQ+POY+ZOY+QOZ=1+3+9+3=16, so area XPQ= 2 units. Area XYZ=9 × area XPQ=18 units.

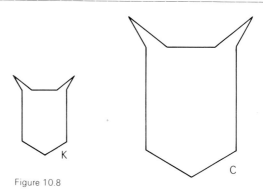

Figure 10.8

Exercise 10.2

1. Use tracing paper to make a copy of the figures C and K. Find the centre and the scale factors of the enlargements that map

   a K onto C   b C onto K.

2. Repeat Question 1, but this time separate the tracings of C and K, and draw K in a different position relative to C (but always 'the same way up', i.e. as the image under a translation of the original position of K). Find the new centre of enlargement. Repeat with K inside C, and again with a point of K coinciding with the corresponding point of C.

3. Repeat Question 2, but this time turn K upside down, so that it is the image of its original position under a rotation of 180°. Find the centre of enlargement. What is now the scale factor of the enlargement? Repeat with two more positions of K.

CHAPTER 10 — ENLARGEMENT AND SIMILARITY

4 Draw the following triangles.
T, whose vertices are at $(-2, 0)$, $(-3, 0)$ and $(-3, 2)$,
U, whose vertices are at $(3, -3)$, $(0, -3)$ and $(0, 3)$,
V, whose vertices are at $(2, 4)$, $(4, 4)$ and $(4, 0)$.
Find the centres and scale factors of the enlargements that map

    a T onto U   **c** T onto V   **e** U onto V
    b U onto T   **d** V onto T   **f** V onto U

5 E is an enlargement with centre $(-1, 1)$ and scale factor 2; F is an enlargement with centre $(-2, 3)$ and scale factor -2. T is the same triangle as it was in Question 4. Draw $E(T)$ and $FE(T)$. Find the centre and scale factor of the single enlargement equivalent to FE.

Draw $F(T)$ and $EF(T)$. Find the centre and scale factor of the single enlargement equivalent to EF.

6 Q is the quadrilateral whose vertices are at $(1, 1)$, $(3, 1)$, $(3, 2)$ and $(1, 4)$. G is an enlargement with centre $(0, 0)$ and scale factor 3. Draw $G(Q)$.

T is a translation with vector $\begin{pmatrix} -6 \\ 3 \end{pmatrix}$. Draw $TG(Q)$, and find the centre and scale factor of the single enlargement equivalent to GT.

7 Q, G and T have the same meanings as in Question 6. Find in the same way as in Question 6 the centres and scale factors of the single enlargements equivalent to

    a GT **b** GT^2 **c** TGT **d** T^2G

8 W is the triangle whose vertices are at $(1, -1)$, $(-1, -1)$ and $(-1, 2)$. H is an enlargement with centre $(0, 0)$ and scale factor 3. Draw $H(W)$.

R is a rotation of 180° about $(2, 0)$. Draw $RH(W)$ and find the centre and scale factor of the single enlargement equivalent to RH.

In a similar way find the centre and scale factor of the single enlargement equivalent to HR.

9 Copy Figure 10.9, and draw its image under an enlargement with scale factor 2 and any convenient centre. What is the area scale factor of the enlargement?

The figure and its image might be taken to represent cubes. How many times larger is the *volume* of the image cube than that of the original cube?

Repeat the question, but with scale factor 3 instead of 2.

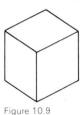
Figure 10.9

10 Figure 10.10 shows a square divided into four smaller, equal squares. Find the centres and the scale factors of the enlargements that map

a ABED onto ACIG
b ACI onto ABE
c ABE onto AGI
d EOB onto AOG
e AOB onto IOG.

In what ratio does O divide AI? In what ratio does O divide GB?

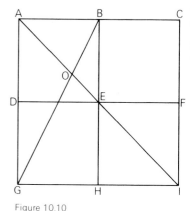

Figure 10.10

11 Figure 10.11 shows a rectangle divided into four unequal rectangles. Find the centres and the scale factors of the enlargements that map

a BED onto HEF
b HEY onto BEX
c ACIG onto ABED
d ABX onto IHY

O is the centre of an enlargement that maps ABD onto EFH.
Calculate the scale factor, and calculate OA.

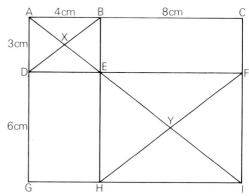

Figure 10.11

12 ABCD is a parallelogram, and X is the mid-point of AB. DX crosses AC at Y. Give the centre, and the linear and area scale factors, of the enlargement that maps triangle AXY onto triangle CDY. Find the ratios AY:YC and DY:YX. If the area of triangle CDY is 8 cm², find the areas of the figures AXY, ADY, ACD, ABC, BXYC and ABCD.

13 Draw a triangle ABC. Draw ARQ, the image of ABC under an enlargement with centre A and scale factor ½. Draw RBP, the image of ABC under an enlargement with centre B and scale factor ½.

Describe the transformation that maps ABC onto QPC.

Show that PQR is the image of ABC under an enlargement. Give the scale factor of this enlargement, and find its centre G. In what ratio does G divide AP, BQ and CR?

(G is the **centroid** or **centre of gravity** of the triangle ABC.)

CHAPTER 10 — ENLARGEMENT AND SIMILARITY

14 In Figure 10.12, PX = 4 cm, XQ = 6 cm. Find the ratios

 a area PXY : area PQR
 b area PXY : area XYQR
 c area XOY : area QOR
 d area XOY : area XOQ
 e area XOY : area XYQR

If the area of triangle XOY is 8.4 cm², find the areas of all the other figures named.

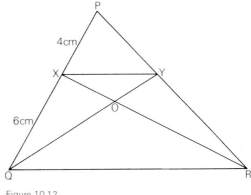

Figure 10.12

15 Draw a triangle ABC. Draw a square with two vertices on BC and one on AB. Hence, by a suitable enlargement, construct a square with two vertices on BC, one on AB and one on AC.

16 Draw a semi-circle with a diameter PQ. By drawing a certain small square and enlarging it, construct a square with two vertices on PQ and two on the circumference of the semi-circle.

17 ABCD is a square and WXYZ is a smaller square, inside ABCD, with W and X both lying on AB. Prove that DZ and CY, if produced, meet on AB.

18 What is the image of a circle under enlargement? If the centre of enlargement lies on the circle, what can be said about the circle and its image?

Two circles touch at O. A line through O cuts the smaller circle at P and the larger at Q; another line through O cuts the smaller circle at R and the larger at S. Prove that PR is parallel to QS.

Maps

A map may be regarded to some extent as an 'enlargement' of the region it represents, the scale factor being always very small — perhaps $\frac{1}{100}$ for a plan, $\frac{1}{50000}$ (i.e. 2×10^{-5}) for a local map, or as small as 10^{-8} for a map of the world. On the map itself these are usually written as 1:100, 1:50 000, etc.

Example 3 The scale of a map is 1:50 000. Calculate
 a the distance, in kilometres, between two buildings represented on the map by dots 7.8 cm apart
 b the length of a line on the map representing a straight road 5.6 km long

c the area of a wood represented on the map by a green rectangle of area 3.6 cm².

Answer
a Distance = 7.8 × 50 000 cm
$$= \frac{7.8 \times 50\,000}{100 \times 1000} \text{ km}$$
= 3.9 km
b length = 5.6 ÷ 50 000 km
= 5.6 × 10^5 ÷ 50 000 cm
= 11.2 cm
c The *area* scale factor is
$$\left(\frac{1}{50\,000}\right)^2 = 4 \times 10^{-10}$$
So the area of the wood is
3.6 ÷ (4 × 10^{-10}) cm²
= 9 × 10^9 cm²
= 9 × 10^5 m² (1 m² = 10^4 cm²)
or 0.9 km² (1 km² = 10^6 m²)

Similarity

If a figure Q is the image of a figure P under an enlargement, then P and Q are *similar* ('the same shape') and *homothetic* ('the same way up' – unless the scale factor is negative). If one of the figures is then 'moved about', perhaps subjected to a rotation or a reflection, the figures may no longer be homothetic but they will still be similar.

If two figures are similar, then

1 all angles in one figure are equal to the corresponding angles in the other,
2 all lengths in one (e.g. the lengths of the sides) are proportional to the corresponding lengths in the other,
3 the areas are proportional to the squares of corresponding lengths.

Example 4 The quadrilaterals ABCD and WXYZ are similar, with $\angle A = \angle W$, $\angle X = \angle Y$ and so on. Calculate the lengths of AB, XY and YZ, the other lengths being as shown in Figure 10.13.

If the area of ABCD is 72 cm², calculate the area of WXYZ.

Answer
Method **1**. We know the corresponding lengths AD and YZ, so the scale factor mapping lengths in ABCD onto lengths in WXYZ is $\frac{6}{8} = \frac{3}{4}$.
So $y = 12 \times \frac{3}{4} = 9$, $z = 10 \times \frac{3}{4} = 7.5$
Also $x = 3 \div \frac{3}{4} = 4$

CHAPTER 10 — ENLARGEMENT AND SIMILARITY

The area scale factor $= (\frac{3}{4})^2 = \frac{9}{16}$,
so the area of WXYZ $= 72$ cm$^2 \times \frac{9}{16} = 40.5$ cm^2.

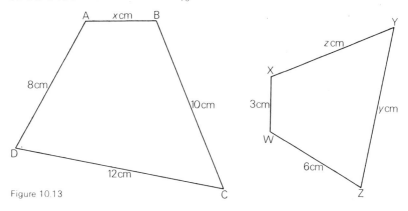

Figure 10.13

Method **2**. Since corresponding sides are proportional, we can write

$$\frac{x}{3} = \frac{10}{z} = \frac{12}{y} = \frac{8}{6}$$

Multiplying these equations out gives $8y = 72$, $8z = 60$, $6x = 24$

whence $x = 4$, $y = 9$, $z = 7.5$.

Area of WXYZ $= 72 \times (\frac{6}{8})^2$ cm$^2 = 40.5$ cm^2.

Exercise 10.3

1 The plan of a garden is drawn on a scale of 1:200. Calculate

   a the dimensions of a flower-bed represented on the plan by a rectangle 3.5 cm long and 2.5 cm wide, (answer in metres)
   b the dimensions of the rectangle representing a lawn 20 m long and 15 m wide, (answer in cm)
   c the area of a border represented by a figure whose area is 24 cm^2, (answer in square metres)

2 A model railway engine is made on a scale of 1:72. Calculate

   a the length of the engine if that of the model is 8.5 cm
   b the 'gauge' of the model, if that of the real engine is 143.5 cm
   c the area (in square metres) of the front of the engine, if that of the front of the model is 3.6 cm^2

3 A map of England and Wales is drawn on a scale of 1:2 000 000. Calculate

   a the distance (in kilometres) from Hereford to Aylesbury, if the distance between the dots representing these towns on the map is 6.6 cm

b the distance between the dots representing Lincoln and Holyhead, if the actual distance is 270 km
c the area of the part of the map representing Cornwall, whose area is about 3.54×10^9 m².

4 A map of the North London area has a scale of 1:50 000. Calculate

a the length, in kilometres, of the almost straight stretch of the Roman road between Elstree and St. Albans (21.7 cm on the map)
b the length, in cm, of the dotted lines on the map representing the Watford tunnel, whose length is 1.820 km
c the approximate area, in square metres, of King George's Reservoir, represented on the map by a blue shape, approximately a rectangle, with area about 7.5 cm²

5 A map of Africa has a scale of $1:4 \times 10^7$. Calculate

a the distance in a straight line, in kilometres, from Ibadan to Mombasa, if the distance between the dots on the map representing these towns is 10.5 cm. Find also the range of possible values of this distance, if the map measurement is correct only to the nearest millimetre.
b the length, in centimetres, of the blue line on the map representing the Nile, whose length is 6690 km
c the area of the blue patch on the map representing Lake Victoria, whose area is 69 500 km²

6 The area of the United Kingdom is 2.44×10^5 km² and the greatest overall length of Great Britain is 968 km. Find the area of the region and the length of the line representing these, on maps whose scales are

    a 1:2 000 000   **b** 1:5 000 000   **c** $1:10^7$ **d** $1:4 \times 10^7$

7 Of which of the following sets are all members similar to each other?

    a {triangles}
    b {isosceles triangles}
    c {right-angled isosceles triangles}
    d {equilateral triangles}
    e {squares}
    f {rhombuses}
    g {rhombuses with angles of 60° and 120°}
    h {rectangles}
    i {circles}
    j {semicircles}
    k {regular hexagons}

8 In Figure 10.14 the pentagons ABCDE and LMNOP are similar, with $\angle A = \angle L$, $\angle B = \angle M$ etc. Find the values of p, q, r and s. If the area of ABCDE is 144 cm², find the area of LMNOP.

CHAPTER 10 — ENLARGEMENT AND SIMILARITY

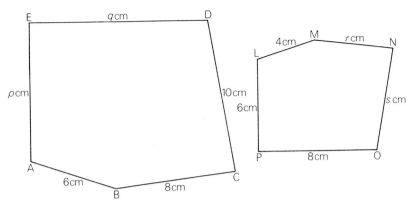

Figure 10.14

9 The sides of a triangle are respectively 6 cm, 7 cm and 8 cm long. Find the lengths of the sides of triangles similar to this one,

  a with the shortest side 21 cm long
  b with the longest side 50 cm long

10 In Figure 10.15 the quadrilaterals QRST and WXYZ are similar, with $\angle$QRS = $\angle$WXY, $\angle$RST = $\angle$XYZ etc. Find the values of a, b, c and d. Find also the ratio of the area of QRST to that of WXYZ.

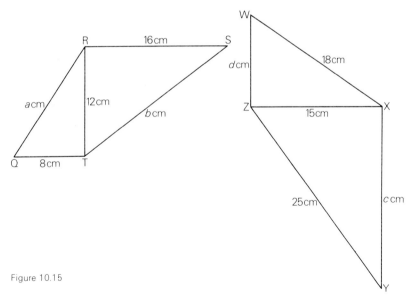

Figure 10.15

11 The quadrilateral ABDC is such that the triangles ABC and BCD are similar, with $\angle$A = $\angle$CBD and $\angle$BCA = $\angle$D. If AC = 5 cm, BC = 6 cm, CD = 12 cm, calculate the lengths of AB and BD. Find also what fraction of the area of ABCD is the area of triangle ABC.

12 In Figure 10.16, the triangles SPR and PQR are similar, with $\angle$S = $\angle$QPR and angles PRQ and PRS both right-angles. Use Pythagoras' theorem to calculate PR, and hence find PS and RS. Show that triangle SQP is also similar to SPR. Find the areas of the three triangles, and show that they are proportional to the squares of the hypotenuses.

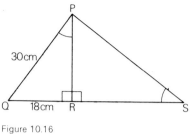

Figure 10.16

13 In Figure 10.17, the triangles WXZ and XZY are similar, with $\angle$W = $\angle$ZXY, and angles WXZ and XZY both right-angles. Use Pythagoras' theorem to calculate XZ, and hence find XY and YZ. Find the areas of the two triangles, and show that they are proportional to the squares of their shortest sides.

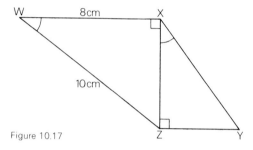

Figure 10.17

14 ABCD is a square with each side 10 cm long, and X is a point on BC such that BX = 2 cm. XY is drawn perpendicular to the diagonal AC, so that Y lies on AC. Show that triangle XYC is similar to triangle ABC, and calculate the area of triangle XYC.

Similar triangles

In order to prove that two figures are similar, it is usually necessary to show that the corresponding angles are equal *and* that the corresponding sides are proportional. However, if the figures are triangles, *either* of these conditions is sufficient.

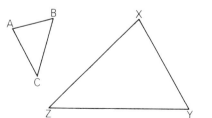
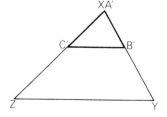

Figure 10.18

CHAPTER 10 — ENLARGEMENT AND SIMILARITY

In Figure 10.18, ABC and XYZ are triangles with $\angle A = \angle X$, $\angle B = \angle Y$ and, therefore, $\angle C = \angle Z$. We will show that the triangles are similar.

By subjecting ABC to translation, rotation and if necessary reflection, we can find an image A'B'C', congruent to ABC, with A' at X, B' on XY and C' on XZ, as shown in the second figure.

Since $\angle A'B'C' = \angle Y$, B'C' is parallel to YZ. This means that A'B'C' is an enlargement of XYZ, and so is similar to XYZ; since ABC is congruent to A'B'C', ABC is also similar to XYZ.

It can be proved, nearly as simply, that ABC is similar to XYZ

a if $\dfrac{AB}{XY} = \dfrac{BC}{YZ} = \dfrac{CA}{ZX}$, or

b if $\angle A = \angle X$ and $\dfrac{BC}{YZ} = \dfrac{CA}{ZX}$

However, these proofs are not given here since the results are not needed for the next exercise, nor for any part of the course.

Exercise 10.4

1 ABCD is a trapezium with AB parallel to DC; also $\angle A = \angle DBC$. Prove that the triangles ABD and BDC are similar. If AB = 3 cm, BD = 5 cm, DA = 6 cm, find the lengths of BC and CD.

2 In Figure 10.19, OR is the bisector of $\angle POQ$. PR is drawn perpendicular to OR, and RQ to OQ. Prove that the triangles OPR and ORQ are similar. If OP = 13 cm and PR = 5 cm, find the lengths of OR, OQ and QR.

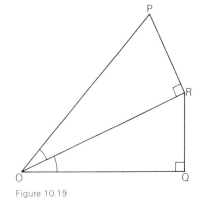

Figure 10.19

3 WXYZ is a square, and O is the mid-point of WX. OZ is joined, and P is a point on OZ such that $\angle YPZ$ is a right angle. Prove that triangles WOZ and PZY are similar. If WZ = 8 cm, calculate the lengths of OZ, PY and PZ and the areas of triangles WOZ and PZY and quadrilateral OXYP.

4 LMN is an isosceles triangle with LM = LN, and O is a point on LM such that ON = MN. Prove that triangles LMN and NMO are similar. If LM = 9 cm and MN = 6 cm, find the length of OM, and find the ratio in which ON divides the area of triangle LMN.

5 ABC is a triangle right-angled at A. D is the foot of the perpendicular from A to BC. Show that the triangles ABC, DBA and DAC are all similar. If BC = 25 cm and AC = 24 cm, calculate the lengths of AB, AD, BD and DC.

6 In Figure 10.20 the angles at P and R are equal. Prove that OP × OS = OQ × OR. If the lengths of OP, OQ and OR are respectively 6, 8 and 9 cm, find the length of OS. If, also, the area of triangle OPQ is 20 cm², find the area of triangle ORS.

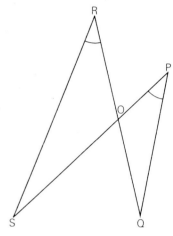

Figure 10.20

7 XYZ is a triangle in which X is a right angle and XY > XZ. The perpendicular bisector of YZ meets XY at K. If YZ = x cm, XY = y cm, find expressions in terms of x and y for

a the length of KY in centimetres
b the ratio in which the perpendicular bisector of YZ divides the area of triangle XYZ.

Volumes of similar solids

If two **solid** figures are similar, then their **volumes** are proportional to the **cubes** of corresponding lengths. If they are objects made of the same material (or of materials with the same density), then their **masses** and their **weights** are also proportional to the cubes of corresponding lengths.

Example 5 A bronze statue is 4 m high. A model is made, also in bronze, and is 20 cm high. The volume of the model is 420 cm³ and it weighs 3.6 kg. Find the volume and the weight of the statue.

Answer

The scale factor for lengths is $\frac{400}{20} = 20$. The scale factor for volumes is therefore $(20)^3 = 8000$.

The volume of the statue is 420 × 8000 cm³
= 3 360 000 cm³ or 3.36 m³.
It weighs 3.6 × 8000 kg = 28 800 kg or 28.8 tonnes.

CHAPTER 10 — ENLARGEMENT AND SIMILARITY

A simple demonstration model

Find two rectangular sheets of paper of the same size and shape. Take one of them and fold it four times, each fold being at right angles to the previous one, so as to make 16 thicknesses. Open the paper out again, and the creases will form 16 rectangles (see Figure 10.21; the dotted lines indicate the creases). Cut along the creases indicated in the diagram by continuous lines, thus forming 8 flaps. Paste flap A exactly over flap B, and flap C exactly over flap D. Paste the other flaps (E in the figure) to A and C where they overlap: see the second part of the figure. You now have a very simple model house.

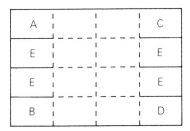
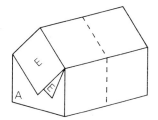

Figure 10.21

Take the other sheet and fold it into quarters; cut out one quarter and put the rest aside. Use the one quarter, exactly as before, to make a smaller model house. How many times larger are the lengths in the larger house than the corresponding lengths in the smaller one? How many times larger is the area of paper used in making it? How many times larger is its volume? You will need to make some measurements and calculations to find the exact volumes.

If there is time, use some of the remaining paper to make a still smaller house; you can go on in this way until the paper becomes too small to be manageable. Each time you make a new house, find the linear, area and volume scale factors between it and each of the other houses.

Exercise 10.5

1   A saucepan of diameter 15 cm holds 2 litres. Find the capacity of a similar saucepan whose diameter is 30 cm.

2   A slab of chocolate 8 cm long weighs 200 g. Find the weight of a similar slab 12 cm long.

3   A paper house, made from a sheet of paper 20 cm long and 16 cm wide, has volume 240 cm³. Find the volumes of similar houses made from sheets

   a   15 cm long and 12 cm wide   b   25 cm long and 20 cm wide

4 An iron casting is 12 cm long, and its mass is 1.6 kg. Find the mass of a similar casting

    a if its length is 18 cm   **b** if its length is 30 cm.

5 A greengrocer sells large apples, of which 8 weigh 1 kg, and small apples, of which 27 weigh 1 kg. If the average diameter of a large apple is 6 cm, find that of a small apple.

6 The greater woozle (an imaginary animal) is 40 cm long when fully grown. Its tail is 10 cm long, the area of its skin is 800 cm^2, and it weighs 2.8 kg. The lesser woozle is similar to the greater woozle, but is only 30 cm long. Find the length of tail, area of skin, and weight of a lesser woozle.

7 In an old-fashioned grocer's shop there is a set of brass weights, all the same shape. The one ounce weight is 1 inch high: which weight is 2 inches high?

8 In the same shop, a supply of butter, weighing 48 pounds, is formed into a cone 18 inches high, and customers are served by removing horizontal slices of butter from the top of the cone. How much butter has been sold when the height has been reduced to 6 inches?

9 Eight lead spheres, each of diameter 10 cm, are melted down and recast into spheres of diameter 2 cm. How many of these spheres will be made? How many times more paint will be needed to paint the small spheres, than would have been needed to paint the large ones?

10 The strength of a girder is proportional to the area of its cross-section. A model of a projected structure is to be made on a scale of one-twelfth. How many times stronger will each girder in the structure be, than the corresponding model girder? The structure is to be built with a safety factor of 4, that is, each girder must be strong enough to carry 4 times the load it actually does carry. What will be the safety factor in the model?

11 A primitive creature is so small that it can absorb all the oxygen it needs through its skin. Assuming that its requirement of oxygen is proportional to its volume, and that the amount that can be absorbed through the skin is proportional to the area of the skin, calculate the percentage of its oxygen requirements that it could absorb through its skin if it were 8 times larger, but similar in shape.

Chapter 11
Statistics

The lady with the clipboard is collecting *statistics*, which here means *information* – in this case, information about the opinions of the people being questioned.

The word statistics is also used to denote a branch of mathematics which deals with *processing* the information that has been collected, often with the object of obtaining results which can easily and quickly be understood. The information collected by the clipboard lady will be processed and the results will show what proportion of the population prefers one kind of margarine, or what proportion intends to vote for a certain candidate in an election, or some other fact of this kind.

A simple and well-known example of a statistical calculation is the evaluation of the *average* of several quantities, by adding them together and dividing the result by the number of quantities. This kind of average

is more accurately called the **mean***: thus the mean of the set $S = \{3, 7, 11, 13, 16\}$ is $\dfrac{3+7+11+13+16}{5} = \dfrac{50}{5} = 10$.

The median Another kind of average is the **median**, which is simply the middle member of the set of numbers, when they are arranged in order of size. The median of set S, above, is 11.

If the number of members of the set is even, there is no middle member, and then the median is the mean of the *two* middle members. Thus, the median of the set $\{3, 7, 11, 13, 16, 20\}$ is $\dfrac{11+13}{2} = 12$.

The mode If one or more of the members of the set appears more than once, the member which appears most frequently is called the **mode**. The mode of the set $\{3, 3, 7, 7, 7, 11, 13, 13, 16\}$ is 7, because 7 appears three times and no other number appears more than twice. There may be more than one mode, or no mode at all.

Note The words 'mean' and 'median' can be used either as nouns or as adjectives, but 'mode' is always a noun – the adjectival form is 'modal'.

Example 1 Find the mean, median and mode of the set $Z = \{1, 2, 3, 4, 1, 4, 3, 2, 4, 3, 2, 4, 3, 4\}$.

Answer
The sum of the elements is 40. The number of elements is 14. So the mean is $\dfrac{40}{14} = 3\tfrac{6}{7}$ or about 3.86.

To find the median, arrange the elements in order of size, thus 1, 1, 2, 2, 2, 3, 3, 3, 3, 4, 4, 4, 4, 4. Of the 14 elements, the middle two are the 7th and 8th, and they are both 3. So the median is 3.

As 4 occurs 5 times and no other number more than 4 times, the mode is 4.

Example 2 The mean age of the 20 members of a class is $14\tfrac{1}{2}$ years: they are then joined by 4 new pupils, and the mean age of the class falls to $14\tfrac{1}{4}$ years. What is the mean age of the new pupils?

Answer
The total age of the 20 original pupils is $20 \times 14\tfrac{1}{2} = 290$ years. The total age of all 24 is $24 \times 14\tfrac{1}{4} = 342$ years.
So the total age of the 4 new pupils is $342 - 290 = 52$ years
and their mean age is $\dfrac{52}{4} = 13$ years.

---

*More accurately still the **arithmetic** mean, but as no other kind of mean will be encountered in this course, the single word **mean** will be used.

CHAPTER 11 — STATISTICS

Example 3 Find a set of five different positive integers whose mean is 6 and whose median is 3.

Answer
As the median is 3, there must be two integers smaller than 3, and these can only be 1 and 2. As the mean is 6, the total must be 30. The total of the three smallest integers is 6, so the total of the two largest must be 24. They could be 11 and 13, or 10 and 14, or any other two integers, both larger than 3, whose total is 24. So one possible answer is {1, 2, 3, 11, 13}.

Exercise 11.1

1 Find the mean, median and mode of
   $S = \{1, 3, 5, 4, 3, 4, 6, 5, 4, 2\}$.

2 Find the mean, median and mode of
   $T = \{21, 31, 25, 31, 27, 21, 31, 25, 17\}$

3 Find the mean, median and mode of
   $U = \{1.4, 2.6, 0.8, 3.2, 2.6, 0.8, 2.6, 1.0\}$.

4 Find the mean, median and mode of
   $V = \{25, 36, 49, 64, 81, 49, 16, 36, 49\}$.

5 In seven cricket matches a batsman, Alf, scores 21, 31, 25, 27, 52, 18, and 37. His colleague Bill scores 0, 1, 132, 6, 150, 0 and 2. Find the mean and the median score of each batsman. What do these results suggest about their comparative performances?

6 A group of girls on a sponsored walk collected 50p, £1, 65p, £1.35, £2.10, 30p, 75p, £1.65, 40p and 90p respectively. Find the mean and the median of these amounts.

   Another group collected 10p, £5, £6.50, 20p, 30p, 5p, 45p, 60p and 15p. Find the mean and median of these amounts.

7 Find the mean number of letters in the 24 words of the first paragraph of this chapter (excluding the title). Find also the median and the modal number of letters in the words in this paragraph.

8 In 9 football matches Aytown Athletic scored 2, 3, 2, 1, 0, 3, 2, 2, 1 goals. Beetown United scored 0, 0, 5, 7, 0, 6, 1, 0, 1. Find the mean, the median and the modal score of each team. Which team is likely to have won more matches?

9 Two girls, Alice and Brenda, scored the following numbers of marks (out of 10) in mathematics tests during one term.

Alice   7   8   7   7   8   6   7   7   6   8   8
Brenda   2   10   9   3   10   10   7   3   9   10   6

Find the mean mark, the median mark and the modal mark for each girl.

10 The mean age of 20 boys is 15 years, and the mean age of 10 girls is 14 years. Find the mean age of all 30.

11 What is the mean size of the three angles of any triangle? Can anything be said about the median size?

12 A group of 30 people is asked to contribute to a charity. It is hoped that the mean contribution will be 50p, but the mean contribution of the first 20 is only 40p. What will have to be the mean contribution of the remaining 10, if the target of a mean of 50p is to be reached?

13 A boy has worked 5 examination papers and scored a mean of 34 out of 50 marks. There is one more paper to be worked. Calculate

  a the largest possible value of his mean mark on all 6 papers
  b the smallest possible value of his mean mark on all 6 papers
  c the least mark he can score on the last paper if the mean mark on all 6 papers is to be at least 36.

14 In a normal June, the total rainfall at Sunnybeach is 9 cm. Find the mean rainfall per day in June. In one particular June, the mean daily rainfall for the first 25 days has been only 0.1 cm. What would have to be the mean daily rainfall for the last 5 days in order for the mean rainfall for the month to be 'normal'? Is there any reason to suppose that this much rain will, in fact, fall during the last 5 days?

15 Write down a set of 7 integers with mean 6, median 8, and mode 2.

16 Find 5 positive integers whose mean is 10 and whose median is 15.

17 The mean of 5 different positive integers is 6. What is the largest possible value of their median? Find also the *smallest* possible value of their median.

18 The largest of five odd numbers is 19 and the smallest is 5. Find the largest and smallest possible values of

  a their median   **b** their mean.

CHAPTER 11 — STATISTICS

19 The table shows the prices of some articles in 1979 and 1982.

Article	Price in 1979	Price in 1982
A	£5	£7
B	£1	£1.80
C	£4	£5

Find
a the percentage increase in the price of each separate article
b the mean of these percentage increases
c the mean of the three prices in 1979
d the mean of the three prices in 1982
e the percentage increase in the mean

Are the answers to **b** and **e** the same?

20 Three circles, P, Q and R have radii 2 cm, 4 cm and 9 cm respectively. The radius of another circle, S, is the mean of the radii of P, Q and R. Find out whether

a the circumference of S is the mean of the circumferences of P, Q and R
b the area of S is the mean of the areas of P, Q and R

21 Find

a the mean of the squares,
b the square of the mean of the set {1, 2, 3, 4, 5}. Find expressions for the mean of the squares and for the square of the mean of two numbers x and y. Show that one of these two quantities must always be larger than the other. Which is it?

22 The mean of the quantities a, b and c is m. Find the mean of each of the following sets of quantities in terms of m, wherever this is possible. For any set for which it is not possible, say so.

a $a+10, b+10, c+10$ **c** a^2, b^2, c^2 **e** $a+b, b+c, c+a$
b $3a, 3b, 3c$ **d** $\frac{1}{2}a, \frac{1}{2}b, \frac{1}{2}c$ **f** $\frac{1}{a}, \frac{1}{b}, \frac{1}{c}$

Short methods for finding the mean

It often happens that the quantities whose mean is to be found lie fairly close together. For example, suppose the mean age of a group of children is to be found, and their separate ages are 12 y 3 months, 12 y 5 months, 12 y 9 months, 12 y 6 months, 12 y 0 months, 12 y 8 months, 13 y 1 month, and 11 y 11 months. Since nearly all are 12 years and some months old, ignore the 12 years and find the mean of the odd months only. 13 y 1 month can be regarded as 12 y 13 months, and 11 y 11 months as 12 y −1 month. The total of the odd months is $3+5+9+6+0+8+13-1=43$, so the mean of these is $\frac{43}{8}=5$ to the nearest month. The mean age to the nearest month is therefore 12 y 5 months.

Estimated mean

The same idea can be extended and the amount of calculation reduced further, by choosing an 'estimated mean' somewhere near where the actual mean is expected to be, as in the following example.

Example 4 Find the mean of 34, 56, 29, 73, 92, 61, 48, 77, 69 and 81.

Answer
Estimate the mean as 60, and write down the amounts by which the members of the set differ from 60, writing + for those above and − for those below 60. These 'deviations' are −26, −4, −31, +13, +32, +1, −12, +17, +9 and +21. The total of these is 20, so the mean of the deviations' is $\frac{20}{10}=2$. The mean of the members of the set is therefore 62.

Exercise 11.2

1 Use the above method to find the mean age of a class of children whose separate ages are:

Years	Months	Years	Months
11	5	11	8
11	2	11	10
11	7	11	9
12	0	11	6
10	10	11	4
11	1	12	1

2 Find the mean of the set {2, 5, 7, 4, 6, 3} and use it to find the means of the following sets

  a {832, 835, 837, 834, 836, 833}
  b {4, 10, 14, 8, 12, 6}
  c {7.2, 7.5, 7.7, 7.4, 7.6, 7.3}
  d {98, 95, 93, 96, 94, 97}

3 Use an estimated mean to find the mean of {37, 42, 46, 39, 49, 32, 50, 33, 56, 30}

4 Use an estimated mean to find the mean of {6.3, 5.4, 7.3, 4.8, 6.0, 5.8, 4.5, 7.0}

5 Use an estimated mean to find the mean of {£1.20, £1.86, £2.14, £0.87, £1.50, £1.35, £2.05, £1.90, £1.75, £0.90}

Frequency

When it is necessary to find the mean, median and mode of a large number of quantities, it is best to proceed as shown in the following example.

Example 5 Find the mean, median and mode of the numbers of letters in the words in the second paragraph of this chapter.

Answer
The longest and shortest words have respectively 11 letters and 1 letter. Write the numbers 1 to 11 in a column thus:

```
 1    |
 2    |||
 3    |||
 4    ||||-
 5    |||
 6    ||
 7
 8
 9    |
10    ||
11    ||
```

The first word, 'the', has 3 letters, so draw a stroke opposite 3. The second word, 'word', has 4 letters, so draw a stroke opposite 4. The next word has 10 letters, so a stroke is drawn opposite 10, and so on. The table above shows the position when the first 22 words have been counted (as far as 'collected'); it is convenient to draw the fifth stroke across the first four, as is seen opposite '4', as this makes the final counting easier.

When all the words have been counted, the totals are entered in a column as shown below: these totals are called the *frequencies* of the various numbers of letters in the words. It will be seen that the frequency of one-letter words is 2, that of two-letter words is 15, and so on.

Number of letters (x)	Frequency (f)	fx
1	2	2
2	15	30
3	13	39
4	18	72
5	5	25
6	4	24
7	6	42
8	1	8
9	8	72
10	6	60
11	3	33

It can now be seen that the mode is 4, since 4 letters has the highest frequency, namely 18.

The median can also be found: the total of the frequency column is 81, showing that there are 81 words in the paragraph. The median will therefore be the 41st word in order of length. The top entries in the frequency column show that the 2 shortest words have 1 letter each, the 17 shortest words have 1 or 2 letters each, and so on. The 30 shortest words have 1, 2 or 3 letters, so the 30th shortest word has 3 letters. The 31st, 32nd, and so on up to the 48th have 4 letters, and the 41st is one of these, so the median is 4.

In order to calculate the mean, the third column is used; in this, the number of letters, x, in the first column, is multiplied by the frequency, f, in the second. The first entry in this column, 2, shows that the 2 one-letter words contain a total of 2 letters; the second entry, 30, shows that the 15 two-letter words contain a total of 30 letters, and so on. The total of the third column is now found; this is 407, showing that the total number of letters is 407. Finally, this total is divided by the number of words, 81, giving the mean. 407 divided by 81 gives about 5.002, so the mean may be taken as 5.

Frequency graph

A *frequency graph* can be drawn, plotting the frequency of each number (vertically) against the number itself (horizontally). This is usually a bar graph, as shown in Figure 11.1.

The graph shows clearly the 'frequency distribution', that is, how the frequency varies according to the number of letters. The second peak at 9 and 10 letters is shown clearly by the graph, but is not indicated by the averages, except that some hint of it is given by the fact that the mean is larger than the mode and the median.

CHAPTER 11 — STATISTICS

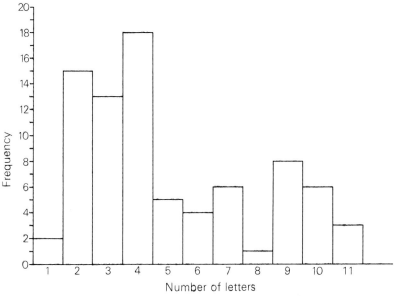

Figure 11.1

Estimated mean   An estimated mean can be used in a calculation for finding the mean of numbers given in the form of a frequency distribution, as is shown by the following example.

Example 6   Find the mean number of matches in 70 boxes with the following frequency distribution:

Number of matches (x)	46	47	48	49	50	51	52	53
Frequency (f), i.e. number of boxes	2	4	12	17	14	12	6	3
Deviation above an estimated mean 50, $d = x - 50$	−4	−3	−2	−1	0	1	2	3
fd	−8	−12	−24	−17	0	12	12	9

The total of the fd row is −28, so the mean deviation is $-\dfrac{28}{70} = -0.4$, and the mean is $50 - 0.4 = 49.6$.

Exercise 11.3

1 Find the mean, median and modal numbers of letters in the words of the paragraph on page 112 beginning 'The graph shows clearly', and draw a frequency graph. (Treat the 9 and 10 as though they had been written 'nine' and 'ten').

2 The following table shows the numbers of people living in the 50 houses in a certain street.

Number of people	1	2	3	4	5	6	7	More than 7
Frequency (number of houses)	6	10	20	8	3	2	1	0

State the modal number of people per house, find the median, calculate the mean, and draw a frequency graph.

3 The following table shows the numbers of pets owned by 30 children.

Number of pets	0	1	2	3	4	5	More than 5
Frequency (number of children)	8	10	5	5	1	1	0

State the modal number of pets per child, find the median, calculate the mean, and draw a frequency graph.

4 The following table shows the numbers of O-level subjects passed by the 60 candidates from a certain school at one examination. No candidate passed in more than 8 subjects.

Number of subjects	0	1	2	3	4	5	6	7	8
Frequency (number of candidates)	2	3	2	11	15	18	6	2	1

State the modal number of subjects per candidate, find the median, calculate the mean, and draw a frequency graph.

5 At a fete, 100 people were asked to guess the number of sweets in a bottle. The distribution of the answers given was as follows.

Guessed number	26	27	28	29	30	31	32	33	34	35
Frequency	3	7	2	10	23	16	10	20	8	1

Find the median and the mean of this distribution, and draw a frequency graph.

CHAPTER 11 — STATISTICS

Statistical projects Carry out some of the following statistical projects, either on your own or as one of a team, as the teacher may direct. In each case, proceed as follows.

1 Decide what set of numbers is likely to be involved, and write the numbers in a column, as in Example 5, page 111.

2 Carry out the operation described, drawing a stroke opposite the number corresponding to each result, again as shown in Example 5.

3 Add up the strokes to find the frequency of each number.

4 State the modal number.

5 Find the median.

6 Calculate the mean.

7 Draw a frequency graph.

It is always more interesting to compare the results from two sets of readings, made under slightly different conditions. The two frequency graphs can be drawn on the same axes but in different colours, if this is thought to be better, and to make comparison easier.

1 *Lengths of words* This is the same project as is described in Example 5, but using other books. Compare one book with another – perhaps a children's book with an advanced technical book, or two books in different languages.

2 *Frequency of an individual letter* Choose a letter of the alphabet, (it should be a very common letter such as E, A or T) and a passage of writing, and investigate the frequencies of words containing the chosen letter 0, 1, 2, 3... times. Compare one letter with another.

3 *Coins, dice and drawing pins* Take a number of coins (four or five will do very well) and toss them all at once many times over, each time recording the number of coins that come up heads. Drawing-pins may be used instead of coins, the number that fall point uppermost being recorded. Or, again, dice may be used; in this case the number of sixes can be recorded, or the number of 'wins', where a 'win' means a score of either 6 or 5.

4 *Football scores* If a newspaper with a number of football results is available, make an investigation into the frequencies of numbers of goals scored by individual teams. Compare home teams with away teams, or winning teams with losing teams (and perhaps with drawing teams also).

5 *Sizes of families* Find the number of members of the family (or the number of people living in the house) of each member of the class.

6 Pets, etc. Carry out an investigation, like the one whose results are recorded in Question 4 of Exercise 11.3, into the number of pets owned by each member of your class. Compare the results with those obtained from another class, or results from boys with those from girls if your school is a mixed one. The same sort of investigation could be carried out into numbers of periodicals taken, numbers of records owned, etc.

7 Estimates Put a number of objects into a glass jar, and get people to estimate the number (as in Question 5 of Exercise 11.3). Compare the estimates of older people with those of younger ones, or those of boys with those of girls.

8 Absence from school If you can have access to the school registers, make investigations of **a** the number of pupils absent each day (the frequencies being the number of days when no-one is absent, the number when 1 is absent, and so on), **b** the lengths in days of spells of absence. Compare one form with another, or boys with girls.

9 Cars Find the ages in years of a group of cars (the age can be worked out from the registration number). Compare one group of cars with another, perhaps the cars belonging to the staff of your school with a similar number seen travelling past the school.

10 Numbers of people in cars Note the numbers of people in cars passing a certain point. Compare one road with another, or one time of day with another.

You will probably be able to think of many other ideas for yourself, but do not choose a project where you have to find the frequencies of too many different numbers. For example, cricket scores are unsuitable for the kind of investigation described in this chapter, because a batsman's score may be anything from 0 to more than 200, and to find and work with the frequencies of all these numbers would be far too laborious.

Chapter 12
More sets

The picture illustrates an imaginary situation when the police of a certain country suspect that a crime has been committed by a man who is bald-headed or bearded or both. They have sorted the suspects into bald and bearded, but some are both bald and bearded.

Two sets which have some elements in common are said to *intersect*, and the elements that are common to both sets form the *intersection set* (often simply called the intersection) of the two. The symbol ∩ is used thus:

{bald-headed men}∩{bearded men}={bald-headed, bearded men}

or again:

{letters of BALD}∩{letters of BEARD}={letters of BAD}

The symbol ∩ is sometimes pronounced 'cap'. If two sets have no elements in common, their intersection set is empty, as in

{A, B, C} ∩ {X, Y, Z} = ∅

If one set is a subset of another, the intersection set of the two consists of the subset, as its members do belong to both sets, as in

{cats} ∩ {animals} = {cats}

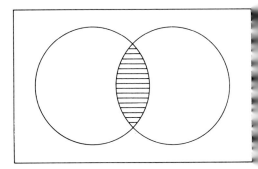

Figure 12.1 shows a Venn diagram of two intersecting sets. The shaded area represents the intersection set.

Figure 12.1

Example 1 If $A = \{1, 2, 3, 4\}$ and $B = \{1, 3, 5, 7\}$
a list the set $A \cap B$
b find the largest possible number of members of $A \cap C$, if C is a set such that $B \cap C = \emptyset$.

Answer
a $A \cap B = \{1, 3\}$, since 1 and 3 are the only numbers that belong to both A and B.
b C cannot contain 1 or 3, since $B \cap C = \emptyset$; the only other two members of A are 2 and 4, and C may contain these. In this case $A \cap C = \{2, 4\}$ and the answer is two.

Exercise 12.1

1 In each of the following cases, give in title form the set $A \cap B$.
   a $A = \{\text{cats}\}$, $B = \{\text{black animals}\}$
   b $A = \{\text{red balls}\}$, $B = \{\text{cricket balls}\}$
   c $A = \{\text{girls whose first name is Ann}\}$
      $B = \{\text{girls whose surname is Brown}\}$
   d $A = \{\text{letters of BREAD}\}$, $B = \{\text{letters of BUTTER}\}$
   e $A = \{\text{words beginning with T}\}$
      $B = \{\text{words ending with E}\}$
   f $A = \{\text{even numbers}\}$, $B = \{\text{multiples of 3}\}$
   g $A = \{\text{short people}\}$, $B = \{\text{fat people}\}$
   h $A = \{\text{trees}\}$, $B = \{\text{oak trees}\}$

CHAPTER 12 — MORE SETS 119

    i A={rectangles 5 cm long}
       B={rectangles 4 cm wide}
    j A={rectangles}, B={rhombuses}
    k A={quadrilaterals}, B={parallelograms}
    l A={factors of 12}, B={factors of 20}

2 If C={letters of SET}, give in list form the set $C \cap D$ in each of the following cases.
    a D={letters of SEND}
    b D={letters of FIVE}
    c D={letters of INTERSECT}
    d D={letters of FOUR}
    e D={letters of SEES}

3 Write in list form the set $X \cap Y$ in each of the following cases, if $\mathscr{E}$={positive integers less than 31}

    a X={odd numbers}, Y={multiples of 5}
    b X={multiples of 3}, Y={multiples of 6}
    c X={odd numbers}, Y={multiples of 6}
    d X={factors of 20}, Y={factors of 30}
    e X={prime numbers}, Y={even numbers}
    f X={even numbers}, Y={numbers less than 13}

4 If $\mathscr{E}$={points in the coordinate plane}
P={points on the line $x=3$}
Q={points on the line $y=2$}
R={points on the line $y=5$}
S={points on the line $x=y$}
name the members of

    a $P \cap Q$ **b** $P \cap R$ **c** $P \cap S$ **d** $Q \cap R$ **e** $Q \cap S$ **f** $R \cap S$

5 If $\mathscr{E}$={letters of MATHEMATICS}
X={letters of HEAT}
Y={letters of MICE}

    a how many members has $X \cap Y$?
    b If Z is a set such that $X \cap Z = H$
and $Y \cap Z = M$, give Z in list form
(i) if it has the largest possible number of members,
(ii) if it has the smallest possible number of members.

6 Each of the three sets A, B and C intersects the other two. Draw a Venn diagram to represent the three sets. Shade in one way the region representing $A \cap B$, and in another way the region representing $A \cap C$. How have you shaded the region representing $(A \cap B) \cap C$? Is it the same as $(A \cap C) \cap B$?

7 If $A = \{$large boxes$\}$, $B = \{$square boxes$\}$, $C = \{$black boxes$\}$, name the sets:

   a $\{$large square boxes$\}$ **c** $\{$square black boxes$\}$
   b $\{$large black boxes$\}$ **d** $\{$large square black boxes$\}$

8 Figure 12.2 is a Venn diagram showing three intersecting sets of a universal set. What is the universal set? In each region are written the letters which are members of the set represented by that region: for example, U and L are members of A but not of B or C. Give, either in list form or as the letters of English words, the members of

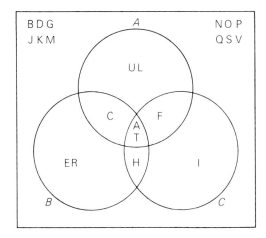

Figure 12.2

   a A **c** C **e** $B \cap C$
   b B **d** $A \cap B$ **f** $A \cap B \cap C$

9 Draw a Venn diagram like that in Figure 12.2, but representing the sets
   $X = \{$letters of HEMP$\}$
   $Y = \{$letters of THEBES$\}$
   $Z = \{$letters of BEAM$\}$
   Give, either in list form or as the letters of English words, the sets

   a $X \cap Y$ **b** $X \cap Z$ **c** $Y \cap Z$ **d** $X \cap Y \cap Z$

   List the universal set (in alphabetical order) if it has as few members as possible.

10 Draw a Venn diagram like that in Figure 12.2, but representing the sets
    $\mathscr{E} = \{$numbers between 40 and 60, both numbers included$\}$
    $P = \{$multiples of 3$\}$
    $Q = \{$multiples of 4$\}$
    $R = \{$multiples of 5$\}$

Union of sets

The little girl in the picture seems to think that what the notice is meant to keep out is $S \cap D$, where $S = \{$smoking creatures$\}$, and $D = \{$dogs$\}$. It is really meant, of course, to keep out all smoking creatures **and** all dogs,

CHAPTER 12 — MORE SETS   121

including smoking dogs, if any. All these together form the *union* of the sets S and D, written $S \cup D$. (The symbol is sometimes pronounced 'cup'). If d represents the little girl's dog, then $d \in S \cup D$, but $d \notin S \cap D$. In the Venn diagram the region representing the set $A \cup B$ is shaded.

Note that

1 the union of two sets cannot be empty unless both sets are themselves empty,

2 the union of a set with its subset is the set itself: that is, if $A \supset B$, then $A \cup B = B$.

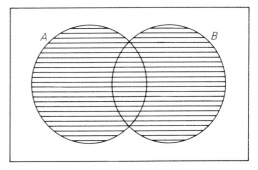

Figure 12.3

Exercise 12.2

1. Repeat Question 2 of exercise 12.1, but in each case give $C \cup D$ instead of $C \cap D$.

2. If E = {numbers between 20 and 30, both numbers inclusive} and
   T = {multiples of 3}
   F = {multiples of 5}
   S = {multiples of 6}
   give in list form the sets $T \cup F$, $T \cup S$ and $F \cup S$.

3. Give in list form $M \cap N$ and $M \cup N$, where
   a $M = \{\frac{1}{4}, \frac{1}{2}, \frac{3}{4}\}$, $N = \{\frac{1}{3}, \frac{1}{2}, \frac{2}{3}\}$
   b M = {colours of the French flag}
      N = {colours of the Italian flag}
   c M = {names of months with 30 days}
      N = {names of months beginning with A}
   d M = {letters of FIRE}, N = {letters of WATER}
   e M = {odd numbers between 2 and 8}
      N = {odd numbers between 4 and 10}
   f M = {Monday, Tuesday, Wednesday}
      N = {Thursday, Friday, Saturday}
   g $M = \{+, -\}$, $N = \{+, -, \times, \div\}$

4. Find two sets P and Q, each containing 3 members, such that $P \cap Q$ = {red, green} and $P \cup Q$ = {red, green, yellow, blue}.

5. Which of the following statements is/are necessarily true?
   a If $a \in A$, then $a \in A \cap B$
   b If $a \notin A$, then $a \notin A \cap B$
   c If $a \in A$, then $a \in A \cup B$
   d If $a \notin A$, then $a \notin A \cup B$

6. If A = {1, 2, 4, 6}
   B = {1, 2, 3, 7}
   C = {1, 3, 4, 5}
   draw a Venn diagram and write each number in the appropriate region. Give in list form the following sets.

   a $A \cap B$ d $A \cap B \cap C$ g $B \cup C$ j $(A \cap B) \cup C$
   b $A \cap C$ e $A \cup B$ h $A \cup B \cup C$ k $(A \cup B) \cap C$
   c $B \cap C$ f $A \cup C$ i $A \cap (B \cup C)$ l $A \cup (B \cap C)$

7. Draw a Venn diagram to represent three intersecting sets P, Q and R. Shade $P \cup Q$ in one colour and $P \cup R$ in another. How has $(P \cup Q) \cap (P \cup R)$ been shaded?

8. Draw a Venn diagram as in Question 7. Shade P in one colour and

CHAPTER 12 — MORE SETS

$Q \cap R$ in another. How has $(Q \cap R) \cup P$ been shaded? Compare your answers to Questions 7 and 8.

Set windows

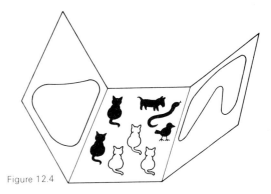

Figure 12.4

Take a large sheet of paper, if possible one much longer than it is broad (a foolscap sheet will do, but a larger sheet is better). Fold it into three equal panels, as shown in Figure 12.4. Choose any two intersecting sets (for example {cats} and {black animals}, as in Question **1a** of Exercise 12.1) and on the central panel of your paper draw some members of each set, including some of the intersection – for example some black cats, some white cats, some black dogs and so on.

In the left-hand panel of your paper cut holes so placed that when the left-hand panel is folded down over the central one, all the pictures of members of one set (the cats) will show through, but no pictures which are not of members of that set. In the same way, cut holes in the right-hand panel so that the pictures of the second set (the black animals) will show through.

When both 'doors' are open, the union of the sets is seen.

When only one 'door' is open, only one set is seen.

When both 'doors' are closed, the intersection is seen.

The complementary set

The set consisting of all the members of the universal set which do *not* belong to a set A is called the ***complementary*** set of A and is denoted by A'. Thus if $\mathscr{E}=\{boys\}$, and $A=\{boys\ aged\ 15\ or\ more\}$, then $A'=\{boys\ aged\ less\ than\ 15\}$.

Again, if $\mathscr{E}=\{1, 2, 3, 4, 5, 6, 7, 8\}$ and $A=\{1, 3, 5, 7\}$, then $A'=\{2, 4, 6, 8\}$.

Example 2 If $\mathscr{E}=\{P, Q, R, S, T, U, V\}$
$A=\{P, Q, R\}, B=\{R, S, T\},$
list the members of

a A' c $A' \cap B'$ e $A' \cup B'$ g $A' \cap B$
b B' d $(A \cap B)'$ f $(A \cup B)'$

Answer

a A' consists of all members not in A, and so is $\{S, T, U, V\}$.
b Similarly B' is $\{P, Q, U, V\}$.
c $A' \cap B'$ is the intersection of the above two sets, and so is $\{U, V\}$.
d $(A \cap B)'$ comprises everything not in $A \cap B$: as $A \cap B$ is R, $(A \cap B)' = \{P, Q, S, T, U, V\}$.
e $A' \cup B'$ contains everything in A' or B' or both, and so is $\{P, Q, S, T, U, V\}$.
f $(A \cup B)'$ comprises everything not in $A \cup B$, i.e. not in $\{P, Q, R, S, T\}$ and so is $\{U, V\}$.
g $A' \cap B = \{S, T\}$.

Example 3   In Figure 12.5 describe how the regions representing the following sets are shaded.

a X' e $X' \cup Y'$
b Y' f $(X \cup Y)'$
c $X' \cap Y'$ g $X \cap Y'$
d $(X \cap Y)'$ h $X' \cap Y$

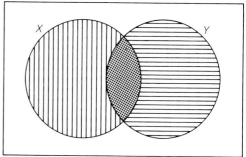

Figure 12.5

Answer
a X' is represented by the unshaded and horizontally shaded regions.
b Y' is represented by the unshaded and vertically shaded regions.
c $X' \cap Y'$ is represented by the region common to those representing X' and Y', i.e. by the unshaded region.
d $X \cap Y$ is represented by the dotted region, so $(X \cap Y)'$ is represented by all except the dotted region.
e $X' \cup Y'$ is represented by all regions representing X' or Y' or both, i.e. by all except the dotted region.
f $X \cup Y$ is represented by all shaded or dotted regions, so $(X \cup Y)'$ by the unshaded region.
g $X \cap Y'$ is represented by the only region which represents part of X but not part of Y, i.e. by the vertically shaded region.
h Similarly $X' \cap Y$ is represented by the horizontally shaded region.

Exercise 12.3

1 Describe A' in title form in each of the following cases.

  a $\mathscr{E}$ = {mice}, A = {male mice}
  b $\mathscr{E}$ = {months of the year},
  A = {the first six months of the year}
  c $\mathscr{E}$ = {letters of CARBON}, A = {letters of ROB}
  d $\mathscr{E}$ = {multiples of 5}, A = {numbers with 5 as last digit}
  e $\mathscr{E}$ = {integers}, A = {integers which have factors other than themselves and 1}

2 If $\mathscr{E}$ = {letters of SECTION}, P = {letters of SET},
Q = {letters of TON}, give in list form

  a P' **d** $(P \cap Q)'$ **g** $P' \cup Q'$ **j** $P \cup Q'$
  b Q' **e** $P \cap Q'$ **h** $(P \cup Q)'$
  c $P' \cap Q'$ **f** $P' \cap Q$ **i** $P' \cup Q$

3 If $\mathscr{E}$ = {integers between 20 and 30, both numbers inclusive}, L = {even numbers}, M = {multiples of 3}, give in list form

  a L' **d** $L \cap M'$ **g** $L' \cup M$
  b M' **e** $L' \cap M$ **h** $(L \cup M)'$
  c $L' \cap M'$ **f** $L \cup M'$ **i** $(L' \cup M)'$

4 In the Venn diagram (Figure 12.6), describe how each of the following regions is shaded or dotted.

  a $A \cap B \cap C'$
  b $A' \cap B' \cap C$
  c $(C \cap B) \cup (A \cap C)$
  d $(A \cap C') \cup (B \cap C')$
  e $(A \cup B) \cap C'$
  f $(A \cup B \cup C)'$

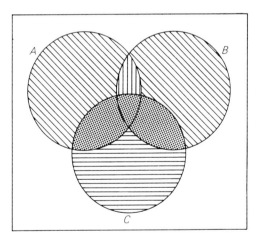

Figure 12.6

5 If $\mathscr{E}$ = {English words}, X = {words beginning with S}, Y = {words containing S}, Z = {words containing E}, state which of the following sets is empty: $X \cap Y' \cap Z$, $X' \cap Y' \cap Z$, $X \cap Y \cap Z'$, $X' \cap Y \cap Z$, $X' \cap Y' \cap Z'$, $X' \cap Y \cap Z'$. State to which of the other sets each of the following words belongs: ASK, HAT, LEFT, SIT, USE.

6 In the Venn diagram (Figure 12.7), region 1 represents $P \cap Q \cap R'$. Name the set represented by each of the other numbered regions.

Name also the set represented by each of the following combinations of regions.

a 1, 2, 4, 5, 7, 8
b 3, 6, 7
c 1, 2, 3
d 6, 8

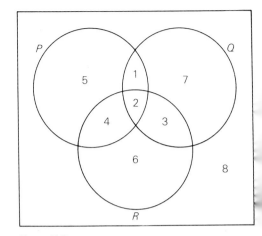

Figure 12.7

7 If $\mathscr{E}$={letters of PARTING}, X={letters of PIT}, Y={letters of RIG}, Z={letters of RAP}, give in list form

a $X \cap Y'$
b $X' \cup Y'$
c $X \cup Y' \cup Z$
d $X \cap (Y' \cup Z)$
e $Y' \cup (X \cap Z')$
f $X' \cap (Y \cup Z')$
g $(X \cap Y)'$
h $(Y' \cap Z)'$

8 If $\mathscr{E}$={months of the year}, T={months with 30 days}, J={months whose names begin with J}, F={the first six months of the year}, give in list form (abbreviating the names of the months if you wish)

a $T \cap J'$
b $J \cap F'$
c $(T \cup J)'$
d $T' \cap J \cap F'$
e $T \cap (J' \cup F')$
f $(T \cap J) \cup F'$
g $T \cup J \cup F'$
h $T \cup (J' \cap F')$

9 If $\mathscr{E}$={1, 2, 3, 4, 5, 6, 7, 8}, A={1, 2, 3, 4}, B={2, 3, 5, 6}, C={1, 3, 5, 7}, name the following sets in terms of A, B and C.

a {1, 4, 7, 8}
b {5, 6, 7}
c {1, 2, 3}
d {1}
e {2, 6, 8}
f {1, 2, 3, 4, 6, 7, 8}

Punched cards

Find some cards; old playing cards will do (but it is best to stick gummed paper on the fronts so that you can write on them), or you can make some by cutting up post-cards, old Christmas cards (the sides without the pictures) or any sheets of card. Write on each card the name of a member of some universal set — perhaps the members of your class, or some books or records you possess. Find also two steel knitting needles, or thin rods of a similar kind.

Cut a row of holes in each card, near and parallel to one edge, and so placed that when the cards are held together in a pack, the holes in each card are aligned with those in all the others, so that daylight can be seen through all of them. The holes must be big enough for the knitting needles to pass through.

Choose a subset – we will call it A – from the universal set, for example the members of your class who play a stringed musical instrument. Take the card of each member of A' (note A', *not* A itself) and cut a slot from the first hole to the edge of the card, as shown in Figure 12.8.

Now choose another set B – perhaps the members of the class who play a wind instrument – and treat the **second** holes in the cards of the members of B' in the same way as you treated the first holes in the cards of the members of A'. Continue in this way until all the holes have been used. If possible, find or make a stand or box in which the cards can be held together in a pack, with the holes lined up.

Figure 12.8

Now, with the aid of the rods, various sets of cards can be sorted out. For example, if a rod is inserted through the first holes and then gently raised, it will bring out all the cards of members of A, leaving those of A' behind. If rods are inserted through both the first two holes, the members of $A \cup B$ (those who play stringed *or* wind instruments, in the suggested example) are selected, and those of $(A \cup B)'$ or, what is the same thing, $A' \cap B'$, will be left behind.

To pick out $A \cap B$ (those who play stringed *and* wind instruments), put a rod through the first holes and lift the cards out a little way, then put another rod through the second holes of the partly-lifted cards, and lift right out all those that will come out.

It is possible to elaborate on this and pick out the cards of a large number of categories.

Sets of numbers

The notation used in this chapter can be used for sets of numbers like those described in Chapter 9.

Example 4 If $\mathscr{E} = \{x: 0 \leqslant x \leqslant 10\}$, $A = \{x: 1 \leqslant x \leqslant 5\}$, $B = \{x: 3 < x < 7\}$, describe in the same way the sets $A \cap B$ and $A \cup B$, and illustrate your answers on a number line. Describe also the sets A' and B'.

Answer
$A \cap B$ consists of all numbers in both A and B, and so is $\{x: 3 < x \leqslant 5\}$.

$A \cup B$ is $\{x: 1 \leqslant x < 7\}$

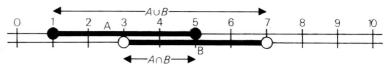

Figure 12.9

A' consists of two parts: one is $\{x: 0 \leqslant x < 1\}$ (1 is not included as $1 \in A$), and the other is $\{x: 5 < x \leqslant 10\}$. We can write
$$A' = \{x: 0 \leqslant x < 1\} \cup \{x: 5 < x \leqslant 10\}$$

In the same way, we have
$$B' = \{x: 0 \leqslant x \leqslant 3\} \cup \{x: 7 \leqslant x \leqslant 10\}$$

Note that $3 \in B'$ because $3 \notin B$, and the same applies to 7.

Exercise 12.4

1 $P = \{x: -2 \leqslant x \leqslant 5\}$, $Q = \{x: 0 < x < 7\}$.
   Describe $P \cap Q$ and $P \cup Q$, and illustrate your answers on a number line.

2 $\mathscr{E} = \{x: 1 \leqslant x \leqslant 8\}$, $A = \{x: 1 \leqslant x \leqslant 5\}$,
   $B = \{x: 3 \leqslant x \leqslant 8\}$. Describe $A \cap B$ and $A \cup B$, and illustrate your answers on a number line. Describe also
   a A' **b** B' **c** $A' \cap B'$ **d** $A' \cup B'$

3 $X = \{x: 3 < x < 5\}$, $Y = \{x: 3 \leqslant x \leqslant 5\}$. Describe
   a $X \cap Y$ **b** $X \cup Y$ **c** $X' \cap Y$ **d** $X \cap Y'$

4 $L = \{x: -3 < x \leqslant 1\}$, $M = \{x: -3 \leqslant x < 1\}$. Describe
   a $L \cap M$ **b** $L \cup M$ **c** $L' \cap M$ **d** $L \cap M'$

5 $\mathscr{E} = \{x: -6 \leqslant x \leqslant 6\}$, $U = \{x: -3 \leqslant x \leqslant 0\}$,
   $V = \{x: 0 \leqslant x < 3\}$ Describe
   a $U \cap V$ **b** $U \cup V$

   and illustrate your answers on a number line. Describe also $U' \cap V$, $U \cap V'$ and $U' \cup V$.

6 $\mathscr{E} = \{x: -5 \leqslant x \leqslant 3\}$, $R = \{x: -2 < x \leqslant 3\}$, $S = \{x: -5 \leqslant x < 1\}$.
   Describe $R \cap S$ and $R \cup S$, and illustrate your answers on a number line. Describe also $R' \cap S$, $R \cap S'$ and $R' \cup S'$.

7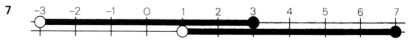

Figure 12.10

Sets C and D are illustrated on the above number line. Describe
a C **b** D **c** $C \cap D$ **d** $C \cup D$ **e** $C \cap D'$ **f** $C' \cap D$

Chapter 13
Factors and quadratic equations

The picture illustrates (not very seriously) the problem of finding the time a projectile takes to reach a certain height: this is one of many problems whose solution involves solving a quadratic equation. However, before quadratic equations can be solved it is necessary to study factorising, and as a preliminary to factorising some revision examples are given of the reverse process, which is multiplication.

Example 1   Multiply out (i.e. write without brackets)

    a $3a(2a-3b)$ **c** $(4x+3)(x-2)$
    b $(3x+4y)(2x-5)$ **d** $(2t+5)(2t-5)$

Answer

a Each term between the brackets is multiplied by $3a$, giving

$$6a^2 - 9ab$$

b Each term between the first pair of brackets is multiplied by each term between the second pair, giving

$$6x^2 - 15x + 8xy - 20y$$

c The procedure is the same as in **b**, giving

$$4x^2 - 8x + 3x - 6$$

In this case the two middle terms can be combined, giving

$$4x^2 - 5x - 6$$

d If the procedure of **b** is carried out, the two middle terms combine to give 0 (i.e. they 'cancel out'), giving

$$4t^2 - 25$$

Exercise 13.1

Multiply out the following.

1. $3(x+2)$
2. $a(b-3)$
3. $c(c-3d)$
4. $2t(t+5u)$
5. $2y(3y-4z)$
6. $4x(x+5y)$
7. $x^2(x+7)$
8. $-3(5-6c)$
9. $-x(3a-4x)$
10. $-5u(-3v-2u)$
11. $(a+2)(a+b)$
12. $(a-b)(x-y)$
13. $(x-4)(x+c)$
14. $(2d+b)(d-3c)$
15. $(h-2k)(3h-7)$
16. $(t+3u)(4+5u)$
17. $(2x-4)(3y+1)$
18. $(2p-5q)(-3p-4r)$
19. $(x^2-3)(x+2)$
20. $(-3-2t)(-2-3u)$
21. $(x+4)(x-3)$
22. $(a+d)(2a+3d)$
23. $(2y-1)(3y-5)$
24. $(b+3c)(2b-5c)$
25. $(4x-7)(3-2x)$
26. $(2p-3q)(5q+4p)$
27. $(6u+5)(5u+6)$
28. $(-3x-7)(4x-2)$
29. $(x^2-4)(3x^2+2)$
30. $(a^2-3b)(2a^2-5b)$

31	$(p+q)(p-q)$	33	$(3+4a)(3-4a)$	35	$(x^2-3)(x^2+3)$
32	$(2x+5)(2x-5)$	34	$(x+7y)(x-7y)$	36	$(-2-3a)(-2+3a)$

Factorising

The reverse of multiplication is factorising. The four types of factorising that will be studied correspond to the four types of multiplication described in Example 1.

1 Monomial factor ('Monomial' means 'with one term'). Example: factorise $6x^2 - 4xy$. It can be seen that $2x$ is a factor of each term, and so is a factor of the whole expression, and

$$6x^2 - 4y = 2x(3x - 2y)$$

2 Binomial factor. ('Binomial' means 'having two terms'.) Example: factorise

$$2a^2 + 2ac - 3a - 3c$$

The terms can be grouped in pairs, and each pair factorised as in **1**, giving

$$2a(a+c) - 3(a+c)$$

As the expressions in both pairs of brackets are the same, i.e. $a+c$, then $a+c$ is a factor of the whole expression, and we have

$$2a^2 + 2ac - 3a - 3c = (a+c)(2a-3)$$

(Note that it is sometimes necessary to rearrange the terms before grouping them in pairs: for example, if $x^2 - 2y + xy - 2x$ is to be factorised, it must be rearranged either as $x^2 + xy - 2y - 2x$ or as $x^2 - 2x - 2y + xy$.)

Exercise 13.2

Factorise:

1	$a^2 + 3a$	5	$h^2 - 3hk$	9	$6xy - 2x$
2	$x^2 - xy$	6	$4mn + 8m^2$	10	$2p^2q - 3pq^2$
3	$3p + 12$	7	$6t^2 - 15tu$	11	$-6a^2 - 9ab$
4	$2c^2 - 8c$	8	$10xy + 15x^2$	12	$a^2b + a$

13	$6x^3 - 3x^2$	19	$p^2 - pq - pr + qr$	25	$4ax - 6cy - 3ay + 8c$
14	$3a^2b + 3ab^2$	20	$t^2 - 6uv + 2tu - 3tv$	26	$xyz - 3z + 2xy - 6$
15	$2x^3 + 8x$	21	$2x^2 + 3x - 4xy - 6y$	27	$p^2 + 3q - p - 3pq$
16	$a^2 + 2a + ab + 2b$	22	$6a^2 + 2ab - 9a - 3b$	28	$a^3 + ab - a^2c - bc$
17	$x^2 - 3x + xy - 3y$	23	$4hk + 8k^2 + 5h + 10k$	29	$x^3 + 3x^2 + 2x + 6$
18	$c^2 + 2cd - 2c - 4d$	24	$6ab - 3b^2 + 2bc - 4ac$	30	$x^3 - x^2 + x - 1$

Factorising (continued)

3 Factorising a trinomial expression, such as $3x^2 - 7x - 6$. The simplest way to do this is by trial and error. Write two pairs of brackets: the product of the two first terms, one in each pair of brackets, is $3x^2$; one term must be $3x$ and the other x, so write these in:

$$(3x \quad)(x \quad)$$

The product of the last two terms must be 6: the possibilities are: 3, 2 or 2, 3 or 6, 1 or 1, 6. Neither 3 nor 6 can be in the first pair of brackets or there would be a monomial factor 3, and we know there is not. This leaves as possibilities

$$(3x \quad 1)(x \quad 6) \text{ and } (3x \quad 2)(x \quad 3)$$

In the first case the two other terms (besides $3x^2$ and 6) would be $18x$ and x, which cannot be combined to make $7x$, whereas in the second case they are $9x$ and $2x$: as $2x - 9x = -7x$, these are the correct terms, provided the correct signs are added. The factors are therefore

$$(3x + 2)(x - 3)$$

4 Any expression of the form $a^2 - b^2$ is a 'difference of two squares': the factors of $a^2 - b^2$ are $(a+b)(a-b)$, or to take a rather less simple case

$$9x^4y^2 - 16z^6 = (3x^2y + 4z^3)(3x^2y - 4z^3)$$

One or both of the squares may be that of a binomial expression: thus

$$a^2 + 2ab + b^2 - c^2 = (a+b)^2 - c^2$$
$$= (a+b+c)(a+b-c)$$

Exercise 13.3

Factorise:

1 $x^2 + 5x + 6$ **2** $x^2 + 3x + 2$ **3** $x^2 + 2x - 3$

CHAPTER 13 — FACTORS AND QUADRATIC EQUATIONS 133

4	x^2+x-6	17	$2x^2+9x+4$	30	x^4-16
5	$x^2-7x+10$	18	$3x^2-17x+10$	31	$4a^2-b^2c^2$
6	x^2+x-12	19	$3x^2-5x-2$	32	$25-9a^2b^2c^2$
7	x^2-7x+6	20	$2x^2-3x-5$	33	$(x+y)^2-z^2$
8	x^2+4x-5	21	$2x^2-7x+6$	34	$(a+b)^2-(c+d)^2$
9	x^2-6x+9	22	$6x^2+x-1$	35	$x^2+2xy+y^2-4$
10	x^2+5x+4	23	$3x^2+x-10$	36	$p^2+2pq+q^2-r^2$
11	x^2+2x-8	24	$4x^2-12x+9$	37	$a^2+4ab+4b^2-c^2$
12	$x^2-8x+15$	25	$15x^2+16x-15$	38	$t^2+6t+9-u^2$
13	x^2-x-20	26	a^2-9	39	$2ax^2-8a^3$ (two stages)
14	$2x^2-5x-3$	27	c^2-4d^2	40	$12c^3-27cd^2$
15	$2x^2-5x+3$	28	$4x^2-25y^2$		
16	$2x^2-x-10$	29	$t^2u^2-9v^2$		

Quadratic equations

An equation containing the *square* of the unknown quantity is called a *quadratic* equation. A typical quadratic equation is

$$x^2-4x-5=0 \qquad \qquad \ldots 1$$

This can be factorised as

$$(x-5)(x+1)=0$$

If the product of two factors is 0, this can only be because one of the factors is itself 0, so *either* $x-5=0$ *or* $x+1=0$, giving $x=5$ or $x=-1$. Both values saitsfy the equation:
if $x=5$, then $x^2-4x-5=25-20-5=0$
and if $x=-1$, then $x^2-4x-5=1+4-5=0$.

Nearly all the quadratic equations that will be encountered in this chapter have two solutions.

An equation which is *not* in the form of equation **1** above, must be put into this form before any factorising is done: see Examples 2 and 3 below.

Solution sets The set of all solutions of an equation is called its *solution set*. The solution set of a quadratic equation may have two members or (more rarely) one, or none at all.*

For example, $x^2+2=0$ obviously has no solution and so its solution set is empty.

An equation which cannot be factorised may nevertheless have real solutions; such equations will be considered in a later chapter.

Example 2 Solve $(x+2)(x-3)=14$

Answer
The left hand side being in factors is no help, because the right hand side is not 0: the left hand side must be multiplied out, giving

$$x^2-x-6=14$$

whence $x^2-x-20=0$

The equation can now be factorised, giving

$$(x+4)(x-5)=0$$

and $x=-4$ or 5

Example 3 Find the solution set of $(x-3)^2+(x-2)^2=(x-1)^2$

Answer
Squaring the expressions in the brackets gives

$$x^2-6x+9+x^2-4x+4=x^2-2x+1$$

This leads to $x^2-8x+12=0$

so $(x-6)(x-2)=0$

$x-6=0$ or $x-2=0$

and the solution set is $\{6, 2\}$.

Exercise 13.4

Find the solution sets of the following equations.

1 $x^2-3x+2=0$

2 $x^2-5x=0$

3 $x^2+x-20=0$

4 $x^2-2x-15=0$

* Strictly, one should say, 'may have no *real* members', but students at this stage are concerned only with real numbers, and the existence of other numbers ('complex numbers') will not be considered.

5	$x^2+7x+12=0$	18	$9x^2-12x+4=0$
6	$x^2-4x-12=0$	19	$x^2+5x=14$
7	$x^2-5x+6=0$	20	$x^2-4=3x$
8	$x^2-16=0$	21	$x(x-5)=2x$
9	$x^2+3x-10=0$	22	$x(x-1)=20$
10	$x^2+4x+4=0$	23	$(x-2)(x+3)=50$
11	$2x^2+3x-2=0$	24	$(x+1)(x-4)=14$
12	$2x^2-7x-15=0$	25	$(x-2)^2=9$
13	$3x^2-7x+2=0$	26	$(2x-1)(x-2)=5$
14	$2x^2+7x+6=0$	27	$x^2+(x+1)^2=13$
15	$3x^2+13x-10=0$	28	$x^2+(x-1)^2=(x+1)^2$
16	$3x^2+16x=0$	29	$(x+1)^2+(2x+1)^2=17x$
17	$4x^2-9=0$	30	$(x+2)(x+3)+(2x+3)(x+5)=(x+5)(x+6)$

Problems solved by quadratic equations

Example 4   If a projectile is thrown upwards at u m/s, its height t seconds later is h metres, where $h=ut-5t^2$. A certain projectile rises to a height of 10 m, 1 second after projection: find the velocity of projection, and find when the projectile is again at a height of 10 m.

Answer
Substituting 10 for h and 1 for t gives

$$10=u-5, \text{ so } u=15$$

Therefore the velocity of projection is 15 m/s. Now we have $10=15t-5t^2$. Rearranging and dividing through by 5 gives

$$t^2-3t+2=0$$

and $\quad (t-1)(t-2)=0$

The solution $t=1$ is already known: the other solution is $t=2$, so the height is again 10 metres, 2 seconds after projection.

Example 5 The perimeter of a right-angled triangle is 28 cm, and the longest side is 9 cm longer than the shortest. Find the lengths of all the sides.

Answer
Call the length of the shortest side x cm; then that of the longest side is $x+9$ cm. That of the third side is

$$28-x-(x+9)=19-2x \text{ cm}$$

Then by Pythagoras' theorem:

$$x^2+(19-2x)^2=(x+9)^2$$

Multiplying out $\quad x^2+361-76x+4x^2=x^2+18x+81$

reducing to $\quad\quad 4x^2-94x+280=0$

and, dividing by 2, $\quad 2x^2-47x+140=0$

and $\quad\quad\quad\quad (2x-7)(x-20)=0$

This appears to give two answers, $3\frac{1}{2}$ and 20: however, 20 is impossible as the length of the third side would be negative. The lengths of the three sides are $3\frac{1}{2}$ cm, 12 cm and $12\frac{1}{2}$ cm.

Exercise 13.5

1 The square of a positive number is 6 more than 5 times the number. Find the number.

2 If x is an odd number, what is the next higher odd number? Find two consecutive odd numbers, the sum of whose squares is 74.

3 The difference between two numbers is 5, and the sum of their squares is 73. Find the numbers.

4 The sum of two numbers is 9, and the sum of their squares is 53. Find the numbers.

5 A number is doubled and then squared. The result is 5 more than 8 times the original number. Find the number.

6 A rectangle is 3 cm longer than it is broad, and its area is 40 cm². Find its dimensions.

7 Find the dimensions of a rectangle whose perimeter is 34 cm and whose area is 60 cm².

CHAPTER 13 — FACTORS AND QUADRATIC EQUATIONS

8 O is a point on the side AB of the triangle ABC such that AOC is a right angle. OC is 1 cm longer than OA, and OB is 3 cm longer than OC. The area of the triangle is 72 cm². Find the lengths of OA, OB and OC.

9 The hypotenuse of a right-angled triangle is 2 cm longer than the next longest side, which is 2 cm longer than the shortest side. Find the lengths of all the sides.

10 The perimeter of a right-angled triangle is 15 cm, and the hypotenuse is 4 cm longer than the shortest side. Find the lengths of all the sides.

11

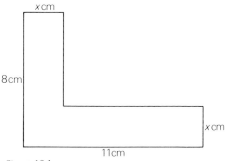

Figure 13.1

12 A projectile is thrown up with a speed of 20 m/s. Use the formula given in Example 4 (page 135) to find the numbers of seconds that elapse between the instant at which it is thrown, and the instants at which it is 15 m above the point from which it was thrown.

13 A length of 100 m of flexible fencing is to be made to form three sides of a rectangular enclosure with area 1200 m², the fourth side being formed by an existing wall. Find two possible sets of dimensions for the enclosure.

14 A circular lawn of radius 5 m is surrounded by a path of width x m. The area of the path is 69% of that of the lawn. Find x.

15 The area of the trapezium ABCD is 60 cm². Find the length of AD.

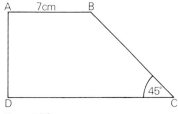

Figure 13.2

16 A square room is extended by 3 m in one direction, and by 2 m in the perpendicular direction. The effect of this is to double its floor area. Find its dimensions before and after the extension.

17 A cone and a cylinder have the same vertical height. The radius of the cone is 6 cm longer than that of the cylinder, and the volume of the cone is three times as large as that of the cylinder. Find the radius of each.

18 The shaded region has four-ninths of the area of the large semi-circle. Find the radii of the small semi-circles.

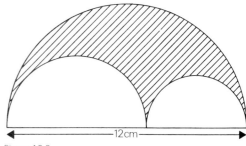

Figure 13.3

19 A rectangle and two squares have dimensions such that the length of the rectangle is 2 m more than its width, the perimeter of the smaller square is equal to that of the rectangle, and the perimeter of the larger square is twice that of the rectangle. Let x metres represent the width of the rectangle, and write down expressions, in terms of x, for the length of the rectangle and for the length of a side of each square. If the total area of the three figures is 53 m², form an equation in x and solve it. Hence calculate the areas of each of the three figures. *(LD)*

20 The price of an article is increased by $10x\%$. Later there is a sale, at which the price is reduced by $20x\%$. The sale price is 28% less than the price before it was raised. Find x.

Chapter 14
Probability

Why do we regard tossing a coin as a fair way of deciding which side is to have first innings, or any other matter of this kind? We can say 'Because it is equally likely that the coin will fall heads as that it will fall tails', but how can we be sure of this? Presumably it is a matter of experience that, in the past, coins have fallen heads as often as they have fallen tails; if heads occurred twice as often as tails we should soon look for another method of deciding who was to take first innings!. But if we toss a coin a large number of times we expect to find that

$$\frac{\text{Number of tossings giving heads}}{\text{Total number of tossings}} = \frac{1}{2}$$

The fraction $\frac{1}{2}$ is called the *experimental probability* that a tossed coin comes down heads.

Tossing a coin is one example of what we shall call a *trial*: a trial may have two or more *outcomes*. The possible outcomes of tossing a coin are, briefly, 'heads' and 'tails'. The experimental probability of any outcome A is defined as

$$\frac{\text{Number of trials with outcome A}}{\text{Total number of trials}}$$

If no coin were available for tossing, would you accept a drawing-pin as a substitute? If tossed it will come down point uppermost ('tails'), or resting on its point and the edge of its head ('heads'). Before deciding whether to accept it, you would need to carry out a large number of trials. Supposing you tossed the drawing-pin 100 times, and it came down heads in 70 of them, the experimental probability of a head would be 70/100 = 7/10, and that of a tail only $\frac{3}{10}$, so it would *not* make a fair substitute for a coin!

Note that it is very important that there should be a *large* number of trials: if you toss a coin only 5 times you are quite likely to get 4 heads, but that does not mean the coin is biased. But if you tossed it 500 times and it came down heads 400 times, you would have good cause to be suspicious.

It can be seen that the largest possible value of the experimental probability of an outcome is 1: this is the value when every trial has this outcome. If no trial has this outcome, its experimental probability is 0.

Another result which is important but easily understood is that if the experimental probabilities of all possible outcomes to a trial are added together, the sum must be 1.

Exercise 14.1

1 A cricket bat is tossed 60 times. It falls round side up 36 times and flat side up 24 times. Find the experimental probabilities of its falling each way.

2 A die suspected of being biased is thrown 120 times. The frequencies of appearance of each of the six numbers on it are as follows:

Number	1	2	3	4	5	6
Frequency	9	18	22	20	21	30

Find to 2 significant figures the experimental probability of the appearance of each number, and describe how you think the die is biased.

Another die, when thrown a number of times, shows 6 every time. What is the experimental probability of each number on this die?

3   Two coins are tossed together 100 times. They both come down heads 22 times, and they both come down tails 26 times. Find the experimental probability that they come down

    a both heads   **b** both tails   **c** one head and one tail.

4   A number of people were chosen at random to answer a questionnaire. The experimental probabilities that they belonged to various categories were found to be as follows:

Adult men (over 18)	0.22
Adult women (over 18)	0.40
Boys under 18	0.15
Girls under 18	0.23

Given that 200 were chosen altogether, find how many were in each category. Find also the experimental probability that a person chosen was

    a over 18   **b** under 18   **c** male   **d** female

5   Two hundred birds from a seabird colony are caught, examined and released. Of these, twelve are found to have been ringed. What is the experimental probability that a bird is ringed? If it is known that 300 birds of the colony were ringed on a recent occasion, make the best estimate you can of the number of birds in the colony.

6   A fair-ground operator runs a game in which players try to roll balls into holes scoring various numbers. During a certain period the frequencies of the possible scores are as follows.

Score	0	1	2	3	4	5	6
Frequency	60	33	21	16	10	6	4

Find the experimental probability of each score. Each player has to pay 10p to play the game. Suggest possible values for prizes to be given for the highest scores, in order that a working profit may be made. (The prizes must not be too small, or nobody will want to pay 10p to play the game.)

7   In another fairground game, two balls are rolled: a black one with which 0, 1 or 2 can be scored, and a red one with which 0, 3 or 6 can be scored. The frequencies of the *total* scores made in a certain period are as follows:

Score	0	1	2	3	4	5	6	7	8
Frequency	72	48	24	16	12	12	8	4	4

Find the experimental probability of each score. Find also the experimental probability of each score made with the black ball, and of each score made with the red ball.

8 An experimenter tossed a coin 80 times, and noted the results as follows (the results are given in the order in which they occurred: H means heads and T means tails). HTHHHTHHTTTHHTTTHTTTHTHHHTHHHT-HTHHHTHTHHTTHHHHTHTTHTTTTTHHHHHHTTTTTHTTHTHHTTHTT

Find the experimental probability of heads, and that of tails.

Find also the experimental probability that, when the coin has fallen the same way twice in succession, it falls the same way a third time. (For example, the third and fourth tosses both give heads, so this counts as a 'trial'; as the fifth toss also gives a head, the outcome is that the coin *does* fall the same way a third time. But the fourth and fifth tosses both give heads, forming another 'trial', and this time the outcome is that the coin does *not* fall the same way a third time.)

Probability experiments

Carry out some of these experiments as your teacher directs. Remember that the experiment has no value unless a *large* number of trials are made: at least 100 should be made if possible. Record the outcomes by the same method as was used for the statistical projects in Chapter 11.

1 *Single coin.* Toss a coin 10 times and record the experimental probability of heads. Toss it another 10 times and record the probability of heads *for the whole* 20 *tosses*. Toss it 10 more times, record the probability of heads for all 30 tosses, and so on until 100 tosses have been made. Plot a graph of experimental probability against number of tosses.

2 *Drawing pins.* Repeat Experiment 1 but use a drawing pin instead of a coin (see page 139). How is the result affected by the dimensions of the pin (length of point, width of head)? Repeat with different kinds of drawing pins, if you can find some.

3 *Two coins.* Toss two coins at once. There are three possible outcomes – two heads, two tails, and one of each. Would you expect the experimental probabilities of all three to be equal? Test your answer, recording the results of at least 100 tosses of both coins. If possible, repeat with three or more coins, finding the probabilities of all possible outcomes.

4 *Succession of tosses.* Toss a coin many times, noting the result of each single tossing as in Question 8, Exercise 14.1. Carry out the experiment described in that question, and find the experimental probability that after a run of two successive heads (or tails), the next tossing will also give a head (or tail). If you have time for a still larger number of tosses – at least 150 – find the corresponding probability for a run of three successive heads (or tails). Do your results give any support to the idea that there is a 'law of averages', which would imply that after a run of heads a head is *less* likely than a tail?

5 *Single die.* Throw a die many times and record the experimental probability of each number. Is there any evidence that the die is biased?

6 *Spinner.* Make a spinner by cutting out a regular hexagon from a sheet of cardboard, marking the sides with the numbers 1 to 6 and pushing a match-stick or other small stick through the centre. Carry out the same trials as with the die in Experiment 5. Is your spinner as fair as the die?

7 *Biased spinner.* Repeat Experiment 6, but this time have the stick slightly off centre, and observe the effect on the experimental probabilities. If you have time, repeat with the stick off centre by varying amounts.

8 *Two dice.* (Or two spinners if two dice are not available and two fair spinners can be made.) With two dice there are 11 possible outcomes ranging from a total of 2 to a total of 12. Are they all equally likely? If not, why not? Find the experimental probability of each total by making a large number of trials.

9 *Football forecasts.* Study any Saturday's football results and calculate the experimental probability that a match results in a home win, a draw or an away win. Try to find a 'model' that will give the same, or nearly the same, probabilities for its outcomes. (For example, if you find that the probabilities of a home win, a draw and an away win are respectively $\frac{1}{2}, \frac{1}{6}$ and $\frac{1}{3}$, you could use a die for a model, with a throw of 1, 2 or 3 representing a home win, a throw of 4 a draw, and a throw of 5 or 6 an away win. Or a spinner could be made with more than 6 sides, some marked 'home', some 'draw' and some 'away'.)

Use your model to forecast the results of next Saturday's matches. For example, if you use a die as suggested, and the first match on the list is Arsenal v. Liverpool, then a throw of 1, 2 or 3 forecasts an Arsenal win, a throw of 4 a draw and so on. Compare your forecast with those of the professional forecasters and, later, with the actual results.

10 *Coins on a grid.* Take an ordinary sheet of graph paper with 2 cm squares, and lay it flat on a desk, a table, or the floor. Roll or spin a halfpenny on it and find the experimental probability of the coin falling completely inside a square. Repeat using 3 cm squares (rule them in ink or pencil), then 4 cm squares and so on. Plot a graph of experimental probability against length of side of square.

11 *An unusual way of finding π.* On a sheet of paper draw a number of 2 cm squares (or other squares or rectangles), placed at random but not overlapping. Calculate the total area of all the squares and also the area of the sheet. Lay the sheet on the floor and drop onto it some form of 'dart'. (A weighted pencil will do if an actual dart is not available.) Find the experimental probability that the dart lands in one of the squares, ignoring any that miss the sheet altogether. Verify that this probability is equal to $\dfrac{\text{area of squares}}{\text{area of sheet}}$.

Repeat with another sheet of paper, but this time draw circles of 1 cm radius instead of squares. Use your experimental probability to find the area of a circle, and hence to find a value for π.

Calculated probability

If we assume that all outcomes to a trial are equally probable, we can calculate the probability of each, or the probability that the outcome will be of a certain kind. We can define this *calculated* probability (i.e. that of the outcome being of a certain kind) as

$$\dfrac{\text{number of outcomes of this kind}}{\text{total number of possible outcomes}}$$

This will be understood more clearly if the following examples are studied.

Example 1 Three cards with the letters A, R and T on them are arranged in random order. Find the probability that
a the letters spell an English word
b the letter A comes first
c the letters are in alphabetical order

Answer
The six possible outcomes are the six possible arrangements of the letters, namely ART, ATR, RAT, RTA, TAR and TRA. In each case the denominator of the probability fraction will therefore be 6.
a There are 3 outcomes of this kind, namely ART, RAT and TAR. The probability is therefore $\tfrac{3}{6}=\tfrac{1}{2}$.
b There are 2 outcomes with A first, namely ART and ATR. The probability is $\tfrac{2}{6}=\tfrac{1}{3}$.
c There is only one outcome of this kind, namely ART, so the probability is $\tfrac{1}{6}$.

CHAPTER 14 — PROBABILITY

Example 2 Two coins are tossed. Find the probability that
  a both come down heads   **c** one comes down heads, the other tails.
  b both come down tails

Answer
The outcomes (2 heads), (2 tails) and (1 head, 1 tail) are *not* equally probable. Four outcomes which *are* equally probable are (1) 2 heads, (2) heads on first coin, tails on second, (3) tails on first coin, heads on second, (4) 2 tails.

The answers are therefore **a** $\frac{1}{4}$, **b** $\frac{1}{4}$, **c** $\frac{1}{2}$. (This will have been confirmed by the result of Experiment 3.)

Example 3 Two dice are thrown. Find the probability of each of the 11 possible totals.

Answer
There are 36 possible outcomes, as shown in the following table.

		\multicolumn{6}{c}{Number on first die}					
		1	2	3	4	5	6
		\multicolumn{6}{c}{Totals}					
	1	2	3	4	5	6	7
Number	2	3	4	5	6	7	8
on	3	4	5	6	7	8	9
second	4	5	6	7	8	9	10
die	5	6	7	8	9	10	11
	6	7	8	9	10	11	12

Of the 36 equally probable outcomes, only 1 gives total 2, so the probability of a total of 2 is $\frac{1}{36}$. There are 2 giving total 3 (1+2 and 2+1), so the probability of a total of 3 is $\frac{2}{36}$ or $\frac{1}{18}$. Similarly the probabilities of the other totals can be found, and are:

Total	4	5	6	7	8	9	10	11	12
Probability	$\frac{1}{12}$	$\frac{1}{9}$	$\frac{5}{36}$	$\frac{1}{6}$	$\frac{5}{36}$	$\frac{1}{9}$	$\frac{1}{12}$	$\frac{1}{18}$	$\frac{1}{36}$

These results will have been confirmed, at least approximately, by the result of Experiment 8.

Exercise 14.2

1 A die is thrown. Find the probability that it shows

  a an odd number   **c** a number which is not 6
  b a number more than 4

2 A card is drawn from a pack of 52. Find the probability that it is

    a a heart   **c** the ace of hearts
    b an ace   **d** a card which is neither a heart nor an ace

3 Use the table in Example 3 to find the probability that when two dice are thrown

    a the total is more than 8   **c** both dice show the same number
    b the total is a prime number   **d** neither die shows a 6

4 Write down the six three-digit numbers that can be formed from the digits 1, 2 and 3, each used once. If one of these is chosen at random, find the probability that it is

    a even   **c** more than 200   **e** a multiple of 5
    b odd   **d** a multiple of 3

5 Ann, Bill, Caroline, Donald and Ethel draw lots to decide who shall fill the last two places on a school outing. Write down all possible pairs of names (there are 10), and find the probability that the two chosen

    a are both boys   **c** include one boy   **e** do not include Bill
    b are both girls   and one girl
                  d include Ann

6 Write down all 12 ways in which the letters of the word POOL can be arranged. If one of these is chosen at random, find the probability that it

    a is POOL or LOOP or POLO   **d** begins with P and ends with L
    b begins with P   **e** begins with P or ends with L
    c ends with L   (or both)
                   f has the two O's together

7 A bag contains 2 red, 3 white and 4 blue balls. A ball is drawn from it at random: find the probability that it will be

    a red   **b** white   **c** blue

Repeat the question for the second ball to be drawn, if the first ball turns out to be blue, and is not replaced in the bag.

8 A card player holds in her hand the king and 6 of hearts, the king and 4 of diamonds and the king of clubs. A second player takes one of these cards at random: what is the probability that the card taken is

    a a heart   **c** a spade   **e** neither a heart nor a king?
    b a club   **d** a king

9 A room has three light-switches (call them A, B and C), which can be switched on and off separately. Write down all 8 possible ways in which

the switches may be set (e.g. all on, only A and B on, only A on, etc.)
If the switches are set at random, find the probability that

a all are on
b at least 2 are on
c 2 are on and 1 is off
d at least 1 is on
e 1 is on and 2 are off
f all are off

10 Figure 14.1 shows a target for shooting. A certain marksman always hits the target, but for him the probabilities of all scores are equal. Write down all possible scores with 2 shots (e.g. 10+10, 10+20, 20+10 etc.). Find the probability that his total score will be

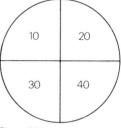

Figure 14.1

a 80   **c** 90   **e** more than 15
b 50   **d** more than 25

11 A heraldic design consisting of a cross on a background is to be coloured. The colours available are red, yellow, green, blue and white. By the rules of heraldry the cross or the background, but not both, must be yellow or white. Make a list of all possible colour schemes (e.g. red on white, yellow on blue etc.). If one of these is chosen at random, find the probability that

a red is used
b the background is red
c red is not used
d white is used
e red and white are both used
f either red or white is used (or both)
g neither red nor white is used

12 Alf, Betty, Charlie and Dorothy are playing Happy Families. After the cards have been dealt, Alf asks Betty if she has Miss Bun, the baker's daughter. What is the probability that Betty has this card?

In fact Betty has not got Miss Bun, and she asks Charlie for it. What is the probability that he has it?

Charlie turns out not to have it either. What is the probability that Dorothy has it?

13 The figure shows part of an electrical circuit with switches A, B and C. Current can flow if both A and B are closed, or if C is closed. Make a table of the 8 possible settings of the switches, stating for

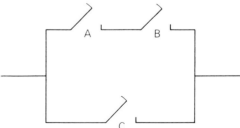

Figure 14.2

each setting whether current flows or not. If the 8 possible settings are all equally likely, find the probability that current flows.

14 A bag contains 10 balls, some black and some white. Four balls are drawn out, one at a time, and all are black. State whether the probability that the fifth ball will also be black is $\frac{1}{2}$, or more than $\frac{1}{2}$, or less than $\frac{1}{2}$, in each of the following cases.

a It is known that the bag originally contained 5 black and 5 white balls, and each ball is replaced in the bag before the next is drawn.
b As for **a**, but none of the balls is replaced in the bag.
c As for **a**, but it is *not* known how many balls of each colour were originally in the bag.

15 $\mathscr{E}$ = {positive integers with one digit},
A = {1, 3, 5, 7, 9}, B = {3, 6, 9}.
A member x is chosen at random from $\mathscr{E}$. Find the probability that x is a member of

   a A **b** B **c** $A \cap B$ **d** $A \cup B$ **e** $A' \cap B$

16 $\mathscr{E}$ = {letters of PROMISE},
C = {letters of SOME}, D = {letters of PIE}.
A member y is chosen at random from $\mathscr{E}$. Find the probability that y is a member of

   a C **c** $C \cap D$ **e** C' **g** $C' \cap D'$
   b D **d** $C \cup D$ **f** D'

17 The following table is reproduced from Question 2 in Exercise 11.3.

Number of people	1	2	3	4	5	6	7	More than 7
Frequency	6	10	20	8	3	2	1	0

Find the probability that a house chosen at random from those in the street contains

a 1 or 2 people   **b** more than 3 people

A person is chosen at random from those living in the houses in this street. Find the probability that this person lives

c in a house with one other person
d in a house in which more than 2 other people live.

18 The following table is reproduced from Question 3 in Exercise 11.3.

Number of pets	0	1	2	3	4	5	More than 5
Frequency	8	10	5	5	1	1	0

Find the probability that one of these children, chosen at random

a has no pet   **c** has more than one pet
b has just one pet

Find also the probability that one of the pets, chosen at random

d is the only pet belonging to its owner.
e is one of 3 or more pets belonging to the same owner

Chapter 15

Trigonometry – the tangent

The picture shows a surveyor using a *clinometer* to find the height of a building. In fact the clinometer measures the *angle of elevation* of the top of the building: in order to be able to calculate the height of the building it is also necessary to know the distance from the clinometer to the foot of the building, and the height of the surveyor's eye above ground level. We will assume that the ground between the clinometer and the building is horizontal.

Having obtained all this information, one way to find the height of the building is to make a scale drawing. Suppose the angle of elevation is 37°, the distance from the foot of the building is 30 m and the surveyor's eye is 1.8 m above ground level.

A suitable scale must be chosen: in the above drawing the scale is 1:500 (1 cm to 5 m). The line AB is drawn, 6 cm long. A representing the clinometer and B the foot of the building. Lines are drawn from A and B making angles of 37° and 90° with AB, and the point where they meet, named C, represents the top of the building. The length BC represents the height of the building: this is found to be about 4.5 cm, representing 22.5 m on the scale being used. Adding 1.8 m for the height of the surveyor gives 24.3 m for the height of the building.

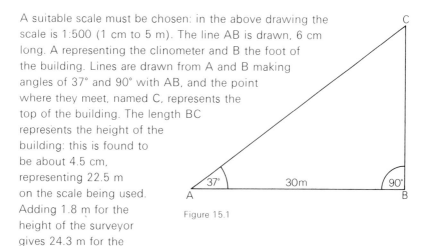

Figure 15.1

Exercise 15.1

Use scale drawings to find the required heights.

1. From a point 20 m from the foot of a building and 1.7 m above ground, the angle of elevation of the top of the building is 52°. Find the height of the building.

2. A surveyor whose eye is 1.9 m above ground level stands 50 m from the foot of a tower and measures the angle of elevation of the top with his clinometer. Find the height of the tower, if the angle is 63°.

3. When the angle of elevation of the sun is 40°, a tree casts a shadow 22 m long. Find the height of the tree.

4. The angle of elevation of the flag at the top of a flagstaff is 22° when measured from a point 27 m from the foot of the staff and 1.5 m above ground level. Find the height of the flagstaff.

A simple clinometer

To make a simple clinometer with which you can find heights to a fair degree of accuracy, begin by cutting out a piece of cardboard the shape shown (O is the centre of the quarter-circle). Mark the curved edge in degrees from 0 to 90 as shown. Make small holes at E, (these will form the 'sighting-tube'), score along the dotted lines from A and B, and bend up the two flaps as shown in the second drawing. Make a very small hole at O and through it knot a length of thin string to the other end of which is attached any small heavy object: this acts as a plumb-line.

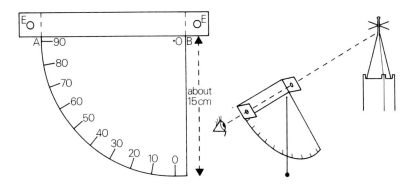

Figure 15.2

An alternative version uses a drinking straw as a sighting-tube: if this version is to be made, the cardboard above AB is not needed and the straw is stuck along the edge AB with sticky tape.

To use the instrument, two operators are needed: one holds it vertically and tilts it, looking through the two holes (or the straw) until the target is seen through them (or it). The second operator waits until the plumb-line has stopped swinging, and then reads the angle shown where the plumb-line crosses the scale.

The clinometer can also be used to measure an angle of *depression*, but then it will be necessary to look through it the other way.

Use your clinometer, combined with scale drawings, to find the heights of buildings, trees and other tall objects in the neighbourhood. You will need a tape-measure, or something similar to measure the distances along the ground.

The tangent

Making scale drawings takes quite a long time, requires apparatus, and unless very carefully done may be inaccurate. There is no need to make the drawing if we can find the information it gives in some other way. All we really need to know is the *ratio* of the height of the building to the horizontal distance measured: this ratio depends only on the angle of elevation and not on the scale of the drawing.

CHAPTER 15 — TRIGONOMETRY — THE TANGENT

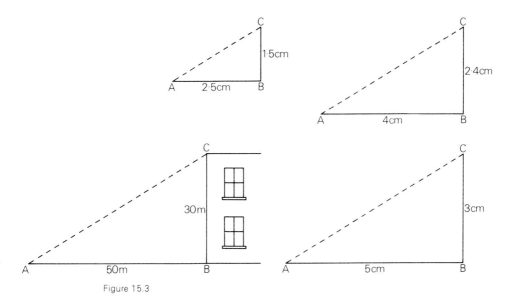

Figure 15.3

Figure 15.3 shows a building and the distances involved in finding its height, together with some drawings of it on various scales: since the drawings are all similar, the ratio BC:AB is the same in all of them.

If this ratio is written in the form $t:1$ (so that for the above diagrams $t = 0.6$), t is a function of the angle of elevation and is called the **tangent** of the angle. Any book of mathematical tables contains a table giving the tangents of angles up to 90°, the angles being given at intervals of 0.1° or possibly of 1 minute (60 minutes = 1°). The use of tangent tables does away with the need for scale drawing in solving problems of the kind dealt with so far in this chapter, as well as in many other problems.

Example 1 Find the height of a cliff, given that the angle of elevation of the top of the cliff from a boat 80 m from its foot is 38°.

Answer
From tables, the tangent of 38° is about 0.781. So if h m is the height of the cliff, we have

$$h:80 = 0.781:1$$

whence $h = 80 \times 0.781 = 62.5$ to 3 s.f. The height of the cliff is 62.5 m.

Exercise 15.2

1, 2, 3, 4 Answer questions **1, 2, 3** and **4** in Exercise 15.1, using tangents instead of scale drawing.

5 Work out the heights found by using your clinometer, using tangents instead of scale drawing.

If possible find some more heights, using your clinometer and tangent tables.

Other uses of the tangent

The tangent can be used not only in solving problems concerning angles of elevation, heights and distances, but also in dealing with other problems concerning the sides and angles of a right-angled triangle. We have

$$\text{tangent of angle} = \frac{\text{length of side opposite to angle}}{\text{length of side adjacent to angle}}$$

More briefly $\text{tangent} = \frac{\text{opposite}}{\text{adjacent}}$. In Figure 15.4, AB is the side adjacent to angle A, and BC is the side opposite to angle A, so $\tan A = \frac{BC}{AB}$. 'tan A' is the accepted abbreviation for 'the tangent of A'.

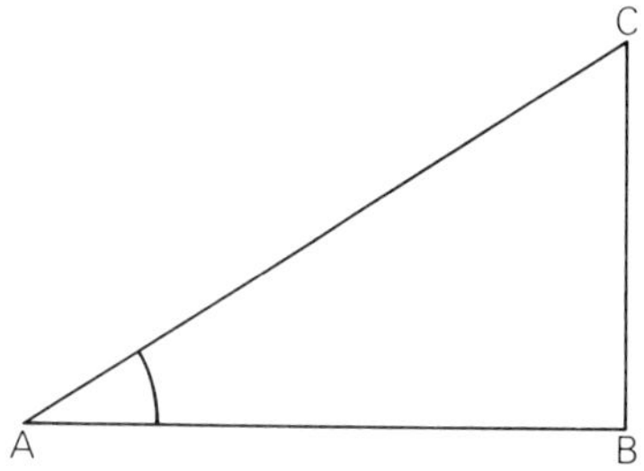

As a mnemonic, remember OAT: this gives **O**pposite over **A**djacent = **T**angent or the equally useful 'multiplied out' form **O**pposite = **A**djacent times **T**angent.

Figure 15.4

Example 2

A ship sails on a bearing 067. When it is 8 km north of its starting-point, how far is it east of its starting-point?

Answer

(See Figure 15.5 below) If the easting distance is x km, then since the easting distance is the opposite side and the northing distance, which is 8 km, is the adjacent side, we have

$$x = 8 \tan 67° = 8 \times 2.356 = 18.85 \text{ km}.$$

Example 3

In the triangle XYZ, $\angle X = 28°$, $\angle Y = 90°$ and $YZ = 5$ cm. Calculate the length of XY

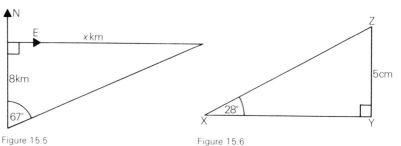

Figure 15.5

Figure 15.6

Answer

(See Figure 15.6 above). In order to avoid *dividing* by the tangent, we use $\angle$ Z instead of $\angle$ X. XY now becomes the opposite side, and we have

$$XY = 5 \tan(90° - 28°) = 5 \tan 62°$$
$$= 5 \times 1.881 = 9.405 \text{ cm}$$

Exercise 15.3

1. In triangle ABC, $\angle A = 24°$, $\angle B = 90°$, AB = 6 cm. Find the length of BC.

2. In triangle PQR, $\angle P = 58°$, $\angle Q = 90°$, QR = 11 cm. Find the length of PQ.

3. One side of a right-angled triangle is 5 cm long, and the angle opposite that side is 41°. Use the tangent and Pythagoras' theorem to find the lengths of the other two sides.

In all questions in this and the other exercises, the ground is to be taken as horizontal, and all walls, poles etc. as vertical unless otherwise stated.

4. The foot of a ladder is 1 m from the base of the wall against which the ladder is leaning. The ladder makes an angle of 72° with the ground. Find the height of the top of the ladder above the ground.

5. A man on the top of a cliff 40 m high sees a boat at an angle of depression of 19°. Find the distance of the boat from the foot of the cliff.

6. Find the length of the shadow cast by a pole 12 m high when the angle of elevation of the sun is 36°.

7. An aeroplane is climbing at an angle of 12° with the ground. When it has reached a height of 1100 m, how far has it travelled horizontally from its starting point?

8. A vector makes an angle of 53° with the x-axis, and its x component is 6. What is its y component?

9. The diagonal of a rectangle makes an angle of 26° with a side which is 7 cm long. Find the lengths of the other sides.

10. The guy-line of a tall mast makes an angle of 66° with the ground. It is attached to the ground at a point 22 m from the foot of the mast. How high above the ground is its upper end?

11. An explorer wishing to find the width of a river drives in a pole directly opposite to a tree on the far bank. He then walks 50 m along the bank

and observes that the tree and pole subtend an angle of 43° at the point where he is standing. Find the distance between the tree and the pole.

12 A road slopes at an angle of 11° with the horizontal, and one end is 40 m above the other. What is the horizontal distance between the two ends?

Finding the angle

Tangent tables can be used to find the angles of a right-angled triangle, if the sides adjoining the right angle are known, as is shown in the following examples.

Example 4

The triangle ABC is right-angled at B AB = 8.4 cm, BC = 5 cm. Find the sizes of ∠A and ∠C.

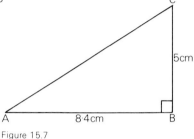

Figure 15.7

Answer
Since it is easier to divide by 5 than by 8.4, we will find ∠C first.

$$\tan C = \frac{\text{opp.}}{\text{adj.}} = \frac{8.4}{5} = 1.68$$

The tangent table is used 'backwards' to find an angle whose tangent is 1.68, or as near to 1.68 as possible. This angle is 59.2°, so

$$\angle = 59.2°$$

Also ∠A = 90° − 59.2° = 30.8°

Example 5

A party of hikers in open country walk 9 km on bearing 340 and then 6 km on bearing 070. On what bearing should they walk to return directly to their starting point?

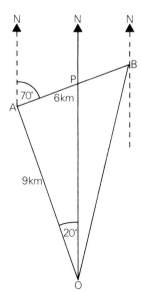

Answer
In Figure 15.8, O is the hikers' starting point, and A and B the points where they arrive at the ends of the two stages of their journey. P is the point on AB which is due north of O.

Since ∠AOP = 20° and ∠OPA = 70°, OAB is a right-angled triangle.

Then

$$\tan \angle AOB = \frac{AB}{OA} = \frac{6}{9} = 0.667$$

Figure 15.8

Again using the tables 'backwards', $\angle AOB = 33.7°$, or 34° to the nearest degree. Hence $\angle POB = 14°$, and the bearing of O from B is 194.

Exercise 15.4

1. In triangle DEF, DE = 6 cm, EF = 3 cm, $\angle E = 90°$. Calculate the sizes of $\angle D$ and $\angle F$.

2. The triangle OPQ is right-angled at P. OP = 5 cm, PQ = 7.8 cm. Calculate the sizes of $\angle O$ and $\angle Q$.

3. Find the other two angles of a triangle if one angle is 90° and the sides adjoining that angle are 6 cm and 9.8 cm long.

4. Calculate the angle of elevation of the sun when a pole 6 m high casts a shadow 10 m long.

5. A rectangle is 8 cm long and 6 cm wide. Find the angles that the diagonals make with the sides.

6. A ladder leans against a wall: its top is 4 m above ground and its foot is 1.22 m from the base of the wall. Find the angle that the ladder makes with the ground.

7. A kite is 25 m vertically above a point on the ground which is 11 m from the lower end of the kite-string. Find the angle which the string (supposed straight) makes with the ground.

8. A golfer is aiming at a hole due north of him and 110 m away, but the ball lands 24 m due east of the hole. On what bearing did the ball travel?

9. Find the angles made with the x-axis by the vectors

    a $\begin{pmatrix} 4 \\ 5 \end{pmatrix}$ b $\begin{pmatrix} -3 \\ 4 \end{pmatrix}$ c $\begin{pmatrix} 5 \\ -2 \end{pmatrix}$

10. A ship sails 5 km on bearing 080 and then 4 km on bearing 170. What is its bearing now from its starting point?

11. ABC is a triangle in which AB = AC, BC = 4 cm and AX = 6 cm, where X is the mid-point of BC. Find all the angles of the triangle.

12. Two points on a map whose scale is 1:50 000 are 2 cm apart. One represents a place 125 m above sea-level, the other a place 255 m above sea-level. Find the angle made with the horizontal by a line joining the two places.

13 The map grid reference of Westminster Abbey is 300795 (that is, its coordinates with reference to certain x and y axes are 30.0 km east and 79.5 km north). The map grid reference of St. Paul's Cathedral is 320811. Find the bearing of St. Paul's from Westminster Abbey.

Further problems

Tangent tables (like Pythagoras' theorem) can only be used in right-angled triangles. If the figure of a problem does not include a right-angled triangle, it may be possible to draw one or more construction lines so that a right-angled triangle is formed.

Example 6 XYZ is a triangle in which XY = YZ, $\angle X = 42°$ and YZ = 5 cm. Calculate the area of the triangle.

Answer

Draw XP perpendicularly bisecting YZ at P, so $\angle XPY = 90°$. Then YP = 2.5 cm and $\angle YXP = 21°$, and $\angle XYP = (90° - 21°) = 69°$.

$$XP = 2.5 \tan 69° = 2.5 \times 2.605$$
$$= 6.51 \text{ cm}$$

Area $= \frac{1}{2} \times 5 \times 6.51 = 16.3$ cm²

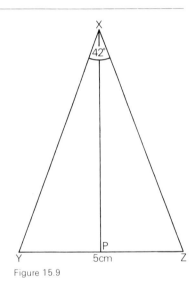

Figure 15.9

Example 7 A lean-to shed is 2.5 m high at one side and 2 m high at the other, and is 3 m wide. Find the angle of slope of the roof.

Answer

Figure 15.10 shows a cross-section of the shed. BX (dotted in the figure) is drawn horizontally through B to meet AD at X.

Then

BX = 3 m, AX = 0.5 m

Tan $\angle ABX = \dfrac{0.5}{3} = 0.167$, so $\angle ABX = 9.5°$

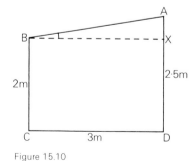

Figure 15.10

Exercise 15.5

1. PQR is a triangle in which PQ=PR, QR=10 cm, and the area of the triangle is 30 cm². Find all the angles.

2. ABCD is a trapezium in which ∠A=∠B=90°, ∠C=51°, AB=5 cm and AD=6 cm. Find the length of BC.

3. Find all the angles of a rhombus whose diagonals are 12 cm and 8 cm long.

4. Find the angle made with the x-axis by the line joining the points (−2, 5) and (4, 7).

5. The line XY is 8 cm long and is one side of a regular octagon inscribed in a circle whose centre is O. Write down the size of ∠XOY. Calculate the perpendicular distance from O to XY, and hence find the area of the octagon.

6. The diagonals AC and BD of an irregular quadrilateral ABCD intersect at right angles at O. OA=3 cm, OB=4 cm, OC=5 cm, OD=6 cm. Find all the angles of the quadrilateral.

7. In Figure 15.11 calculate
   a the length of BX
   b the length of CX
   c the sizes of ∠C and ∠BAC

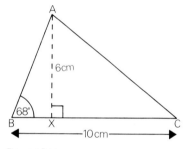

Figure 15.11

8. Two towers are respectively 80 m and 60 m high. From the top of the taller tower the angle of depression of the top of the other tower is 22°. Find the horizontal distance between the towers.

9. When some sand is tipped in a heap, it forms a cone such that the angle of slope of a side is 35°. The diameter of the heap is 6 m. Find the height of the cone to 3 significant figures, and hence find the volume of the heap in cubic metres. (Take $\pi = 3\frac{1}{7}$). (The volume of a cone is $\frac{1}{3}\pi r^2 h$.)

10. From the top of a cliff 60 m high, two boats are seen, both on the same bearing. Their angles of depression are respectively 27° and 41°. Calculate the distance between the boats.

11 The semi-vertical angle of a cone (see Figure 15.12) is 28°, and the radius of the base is 8 cm. Find the height of the cone. Find also the radius of a circular cross-section 6 cm below the vertex.

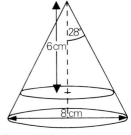

Figure 15.12

12 The ridge of a marquee is 6 m above the ground, the marquee is 6.8 m wide and the roof slopes at an angle of 42° with the ground. Find the height of the side walls.

13 From the top of a mountain whose height above sea-level is 760 m, a hut can be seen at an angle of depression of 23°. The hut is marked on the map as a dot 1.8 cm away from the dot representing the top of the mountain, the scale of the map being 1:50 000. Find the height of the hut above sea-level.

14 A cylindrical coffee-percolator has a diameter of 10 cm and contains some coffee. When the percolator is tilted through 32°, the surface of the coffee just meets the upper edge of the base of the percolator (see Figure 15.13). Find the length d cm, which is the distance the coffee comes up the lower side of the percolator. When the percolator is righted the depth of the coffee is $\frac{1}{2}d$ cm. Find the volume of coffee in the percolator, taking $\pi = 3.14$.

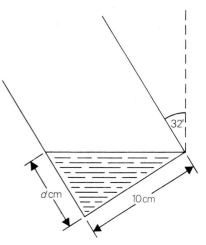

Figure 15.13

15 From a point P on the ground the angle of elevation of the top of a tower is 67°. The distance of P from the foot of the tower is 80 m. Find the angle of elevation from P of a point half-way up the tower. Which piece of information given in the question is unnecessary?

16 From an aeroplane flying on a straight course at a height of 2000 m, a small lake is observed at an angle of depression of 32°. The aeroplane flies straight on and over the lake, and 30 seconds after the first observation the angle of depression of the lake is 67°. Calculate the speed of the aeroplane.

17 A heavy rectangular box, whose dimensions are 1.5 m × 1 m × 0.8 m, rests on its largest face. It is to be moved by rolling it over and over. Calculate the angle through which it must be turned before the diagonal of any face becomes vertical

  a if it is rolled about one of its longest edges,
  b if it is rolled about one of the edges which are 1 m long.

18 The two portions of a step-ladder are hinged together at the top, and connected by a cord attached to points at equal distances from the lower end of each. When the top of the ladder is 1.8 m above the floor, the lower ends of the two portions are 1.2 m apart. Calculate the angle between the two portions, and the length of the cord if in this position it is taut and 0.4 m above the floor.

19 A cylindrical roller of diameter 0.8 m lies on horizontal ground. A rod which is more than 2 m long rests over the roller, with one end on the ground: the point where the rod touches the roller is 2 m from the end on the ground. Calculate the angle the rod makes with the ground. (The rod is in the same plane as a vertical cross-section of the roller.)

20 What is the largest tangent given in your tables? What angle has this tangent? Why do your tables not give a tangent for 90°?

21

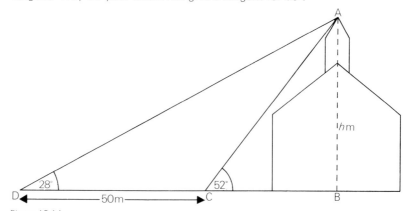

Figure 15.14

A surveyor wishes to find the height of the building shown in Figure 15.14, but cannot reach the point B as it is inside the building. The surveyor therefore measures the angles of elevation of A from two points, C and D, which are in line with B. The angles of elevation are 52° and 28°, and the distance CD is 50 m. Fill in the blanks in the following calculation.

If AB = h, BC = h tan = × h, and

BD = h tan =   × h
DC = 50 m = BD − BC = (× h) − (× h)
 =   × h
So h = 50 ÷   =   m

More clinometer work

If you wish to use your clinometer to find the heights of buildings but cannot reach the points vertically below the tops of them, Question 21 above gives the method for doing so.

Revision exercises

On the preliminary work

Exercise 1S – short questions

1. Express 210 as a product of prime factors.

2. Find x if $3x+2=17$.

3. Two angles of a triangle are 39° and 68°. Find the third angle.

4. Simplify $3\frac{2}{3}+5\frac{3}{4}$.

5. Find the value of a^2-bc when $a=-3$, $b=4$, $c=-2$.

6. Give the coordinates of the point where the line $x=y$ crosses the line $x=5$.

7. Multiply 0.4 by 0.03.

8. Name a quadrilateral whose diagonals are its only axes of symmetry. What order of rotational symmetry has it?

9. Divide £252 into three parts in the ratio 5:4:3.

10. Simplify $3(x-2)-2(x-3)$.

11. Find the perimeter of a rectangle whose area is 42 cm² and whose width is 6 cm.

12. Which of the following numbers have exact square roots? Give these square roots.

    16, 160, 1600, 16 000, 160 000.

13. Given that 1 lb is about 454 g, express 20 lb approximately in kilograms.

14. Multiply $6a^2$ by $3b^3$ and divide the result by $2ab$, giving the answer in the simplest possible form.

15. Divide $3\frac{2}{3}$ by $2\frac{3}{4}$.

16. Taking π as $3\frac{1}{7}$, find the area of a circle whose radius is 7 cm.

17 Find the length of the hypotenuse of a right-angled triangle if the lengths of the other two sides are 0.6 cm and 0.8 cm.

18 The bearing of Aytown from Beetown is 275. What is the bearing of Beetown from Aytown?

19 If n is an odd number, what is the next odd number above n?

20 What is the average speed of a car which covers 210 km in $3\frac{1}{2}$ hours?

21 In an election, 5000 people voted for Black, 4000 voted for White and 3000 for Grey. If a pie-chart is to be drawn to represent this information, find the angle of each sector.

22 Construct a formula to express the following: 'When a small heavy object is allowed to fall, the distance (d metres) that it falls in a certain time is found by squaring the time in seconds (t seconds) and multiplying by 5'.

23 Find the smallest number which is a multiple of 12, a multiple of 15 and a multiple of 20.

24 Taking π as 3.14, find the volume of a cylinder whose base-radius is 2 cm and whose height is 2.5 cm.

25 Find y if $y+3=2y-3$.

26 If $v=u+at$, find v when $u=64$, $a=-6$ and $t=4.5$.

27 AB and CD are parallel lines, and X is a point between them. $\angle$ABX $=63°$, $\angle$CDX$=72°$. Calculate $\angle$BXD.

28 X, Y and Z are three hill-tops. Y and Z are each 600 m from X, and their bearings from X are respectively 090 and 180. Find the bearing of Y from Z.

29 Find the volume of a box 4 cm long, 3.5 cm wide and 3 cm high.

30 Find 35% of £400.

31 Write without brackets $-3x(4y-2x)$.

32 Express $3\frac{1}{4}:4\frac{1}{3}$ as the ratio of the smallest possible integers.

33 Find the number of degrees in each angle of a regular octagon.

34 A girl buys as many identical packets of chocolate as she can for £1. She receives 5p change. Find the cost of each packet (given that it was an

exact number of pence) and the number of packets that she bought.

35 Express as simply as possible
$x^2+4x-3-5x^2-7x+8+2x^2$.

36 Express 54 as a percentage of 90.

37 Give the coordinates of the point which is half way between $(-3, 6)$ and $(3, 6)$.

38 A triangle has n axes of symmetry. Give all possible values of n.

39 The radius of a circle is 10 cm. Taking π as 3.14, find the length of an arc which subtends 45° at the centre.

40 If $8s=3$ and $t=3s$, find t.

41 Find the number of sides of a regular polygon if every angle is 160°.

42 Divide 0.02 by 0.05, giving the answer as a decimal.

43 Find the simple interest on £400 for 8 months at 12% per year.

44 Express 0.030 456 correct to 3 significant figures.

45 Solve the equations $x+y=22$
$x-y=14$

46 Divide £2 in the ratio 5:3.

47 The triangle ABC is right-angled at A, BC=7 cm and AB=3 cm. Find AC^2.

48 The two parallel sides of a trapezium are respectively 9 cm and 13 cm long. Another side is at right angles to both these sides, and is 4 cm long. Find the area of the trapezium.

49 Express without brackets $(a+b)^2-(a-b)^2$.

50 State which of the following numbers are rational: 3, -3, 3.14, $3\frac{1}{7}$, $\sqrt{10}$, π.

Exercise 1A – medium-length questions

Part 1

1. A man invests £2800 in a company and receives a dividend of £210. Calculate the percentage yield on his investment. *(OC)*

2. Solve the equation $\dfrac{3x-1}{5} - \dfrac{2x-3}{3} = 1$. *(OC)*

3. In Figure R1, the angles CAD and ABC are equal, EF is parallel to BC, and AF = CD. Prove that the triangles ACD, EFA are congruent and that the triangle AED is isosceles. *(OC)*

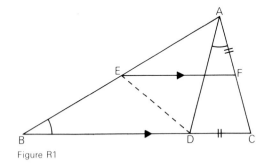

Figure R1

4. Express 15 876 as a product of prime factors. Hence find the exact value of $\sqrt{1.5876}$. *(LD)*

5. A chord LM of a circle of radius 7 cm subtends an angle of 90° at the centre O.
Calculate the areas of the two parts into which the chord LM divides the sector LOM. *(LD)*

6. When the ten sides of a decagon are produced in order, four of the *exterior* angles so formed are each $x°$, and the remaining six are each $(x+10)°$. Calculate x, and hence write doen the two possible values of an *interior* angle of the decagon. *(CB)*

7. A motor car travelled for 2 hours on a class B road at an average speed of 40 km/h, then travelled 285 km in 3 hours on a motorway, and finally travelled 66 km on a class A road at an average speed of 44 km/h. Calculate
   a the distance it travelled on the class B road
   b its average speed on the motorway
   c the time it spent on the class A road
   d its average speed for the whole journey. *(CC)*

8. Plot the points A $(-2, 1)$ and B $(4, 3)$. Draw the square ABCD, given that the y coordinates of C and D are positive. Write down the coordinates of C and D, and those of the point of intersection of the diagonals of the square.

Part 2

1 Solve the simultaneous equations

$$3x - 4y = 11$$
$$5x + 2y = 14$$

2 Evaluate $(\frac{1}{5} + \frac{3}{7}) + (\frac{1}{5} \times \frac{3}{7})$, expressing your answer

  a as a vulgar fraction in its lowest terms,
  b as a decimal fraction, correct to two decimal places. (LD)

3 In Figure R2, ABCD is a parallelogram in which AB = 2BC. Given that M is the mid-point of AB, prove that MC bisects $\angle$ BCD. Given also that $\angle$ ADC = 70°, calculate $\angle$ MCD.
(CB)

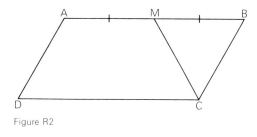

Figure R2

4 The length l of a rectangle is increased by 30% and its breadth b is decreased by 40%. Obtain an expression for the new area of the rectangle. Hence calculate the percentage decrease in the area of the rectangle. (LD)

5 (Ruler and compasses only may be used in this question.)

Construct

  a a triangle ABC in which AB = 10 cm, AC = 8 cm and $\angle$ BAC = 60°
  b the internal bisector of $\angle$ BAC cutting BC at D.
  Measure BD to the nearest mm. (LD)

6 **a** Simplify $4(x-y)^2 + (x+2y)^2$.
  b If $F = \frac{9}{5}C + 32$, find the value of C when F = C. (OC)

7 A bicycle with wheels of diameter 70 cm is being ridden at 25 km/h. Taking π as $3\frac{1}{7}$, find through how many revolutions each wheel turns in 1 minute.

8 Draw a pie-chart to illustrate the following information about the approximate areas of England, Wales and Scotland:

England	51 000 square miles
Wales	8 000 square miles
Scotland	31 000 square miles

Part 3

1 In a certain year a man's annual salary was £6400. He was allowed £1800 of this tax free, and then paid 25% tax on the next £1000 and 33% tax on the remainder. Calculate his monthly salary after payment of tax. *(LB)*

2 Find the value of $\dfrac{4x-3y}{3x+2y}$ when $x=3a$ and $y=-2a$. *(OC)*

3 By considering the area of triangle ABC in two different ways, show that

$xy = h\sqrt{(x^2+y^2)}$

and find the value of h when $x=5$ and $y=12$, giving your answer correct to one place of decimals.

(LD)

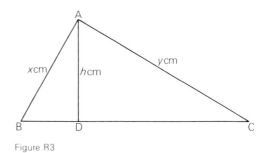

Figure R3

4 Six books were bought. One cost £2.36, two cost £3.30 each, and the other three together cost £6.16. Calculate the average cost of a book. *(CB)*

5 Simplify $\dfrac{(2a-b)^2 - 4a(a-b)}{a^2 - (a+b)(a-b)}$

6 In a parallelogram PQRS, the angle QPS is one quarter of the angle PQR. Calculate angle QPS. *(CB)*

7 OABC is a rhombus, where the coordinates of O and A are respectively (0, 0) and (3, 4), and B lies on the line $x=3$. Find the coordinates of B and C, and those of the point of intersection of OB and AC.

8 A boat sails 8 km on bearing 160, and then 8 km on bearing 280. Find its distance and its bearing from its starting point.

Exercise 1B – longer questions

1 Two children, A and B, were told to find the length of their school field as accurately as they could. They were given no instruments but were told that the distance between two given marks was exactly 20 metres. The number of paces they took in pacing out the given 20 metres and the length of the field were as follows:

REVISION EXERCISES ON PRELIMINARY WORK

	20 metres	Length of field
A	32 paces	624 paces
B	35 paces	693 paces

Calculate the result each obtained for the length of the field, and state the number of significant figures to which the two results agree.

Express the difference between the two results as a percentage of A's result.

In measuring another distance, A took 479 paces. Estimate the number of paces B took, giving your answer to an appropriate degree of accuracy.
(*LC*)

2 During the first part of a car rally, a driver covers a distance of x km in a time of y hours at an average speed of 60 km/h. Write down an equation connecting x and y.

The distance to the finish of the course is then 178 km. He covers this distance in 4 hours. His average speed for the whole course is 50 km/h. Write down a second equation connecting x and y, and solve the two equations. Hence find the total length of the course.
(*OC*)

3 Taking a rhombus as a parallelogram with all its sides equal, prove that the diagonals of a rhombus are perpendicular to one another. (You may assume any general properties of a parallelogram.)

ABCD is a rhombus. Prove that $AC^2 + BD^2 = 4AB^2$. Hence, or otherwise, show that, if the angle ABC of the rhombus is 60°, then $BD^2 = 3AB^2$ (*OC*)

4 Figure R4 shows a cross-section of three solid brass circular cylinders which fit exactly into a rectangular box so that each cylinder touches the other two. The diameter of the largest cylinder is 12 cm and that of each of the smaller cylinders is 6 cm. Calculate the breadth b of the box.

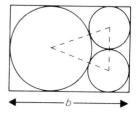

Figure R4

If the length of each cylinder and of the box is 30 cm, calculate

a the total volume of brass in the three cylinders
b the volume of air space in the box.

If the three cylinders have a total mass of 43 kg, calculate the mass, in grams, of one cubic centimetre of brass;
(*LD*)

5 Given that $x = t - \dfrac{1}{t}$, $y = t + \dfrac{1}{t}$, express in terms of t

a xy **b** $x^2 + y^2$ **c** $x^2 - y^2$

and simplify the results.

If $x = 1\frac{1}{2}$, by using the result of **c** or otherwise, find the two possible values of y. (*OC*)

6 Three children, A, B and C, are sharing a bowl of food. When the bowl is passed to A, he always takes one-sixth of whatever is in it, whereas B and C always take one-fifth and one-quarter respectively, of whatever is in the bowl when it is passed to them. If the bowl, which is full at the start, is passed round in the order A, B, C,

  a show that all the children receive equal amounts
  b find what fraction of the food is left when each child has taken (i) one helping, (ii) two helpings.
  If, on the other hand, the bowl is passed round in the order C, B, A,
  c show that the sizes of the helpings taken by C, B and A are in the ratio 5:3:2,
  d find what fraction of the bowlful each child has eaten, and what fraction is left, after each child has taken two helpings. (*LC*)

7 The lines OA, OB and OC are equal in length. AO and OB form two sides of a regular polygon with x sides, BO and OC sides of a regular polygon with y sides, and CO and OA sides of a regular polygon with z sides.

Write down expressions for $\angle$AOB, $\angle$BOC and $\angle$COA in terms of x, y and z respectively, and hence prove that $\dfrac{1}{x} + \dfrac{1}{y} + \dfrac{1}{z} = \dfrac{1}{2}$.

Find the values of x, y and z

  a if $x = y = z$ **b** if $x = y = 2z$ **c** if $x = 2y = 2z$

Hence write down three possibilities for the kinds of polygons that could be concerned.

8 To estimate the cost of providing windows, glazing suppliers measure the perimeter of the window space in millimetres and charge the following rates per mm:

1.25p per mm for glazing with a single piece of glass.

1.5p per mm for glazing with two sliding pieces of glass.

1.75p per mm for glazing with three sliding pieces of glass.

I have four windows which each measure 1200 mm by 1780 mm.

  a Calculate the perimeter of one window.
  I decide to fit two sliding pieces of glass to each of two of the windows.
  b Calculate the cost of glazing these two windows.
  I decide to fit three sliding pieces of glass to each of the other two windows.
  c Calculate the cost of glazing these two windows.

In addition, I decide that a single pane of glass will be adequate for the small hall window which measures 1050 mm by 840 mm.
d Calculate the cost of glazing this window.
e Find the total cost of all five windows.
An extra 10% is added to this total for fitting the windows.
f Calculate the fitting charge.
A discount of 5% of the total price (including the fitting charge) is allowed for a cash payment.
g Find, to the nearest penny, what saving this would represent on this order. *(LB)*

On chapters 1 to 5

Exercise 2S – short questions

1. Give in list form the set {kinds of polygon with more than 4 but fewer than 9 sides}

2. Give in title form the set {2, 4, 8, 10, 14, 16}

3. Name the mapping corresponding to the relation 'is half of' when the domain and range are sets of numbers.

4. Name the image of $(-3, 5)$ under reflection in the y-axis.

5. Name the image of $(-3, 5)$ under a rotation of $+90°$ about $(0, 0)$.

6. $X = $ {letters of CHAPTER} and $Y = $ {letters of ONE}. $P \subset X$ and $P \subset Y$. P is not an empty set: what set is it?

7. Name the mirror line under reflection in which $(5, 7)$ is the image of $(5, -3)$.

8. $f(\text{Fiona}) = O$, $f(\text{Betty}) = T$, $f(\text{Henry}) = N$. Suggest a possible mapping that f might be. What kind of mapping is it?

9. Name the centre of a rotation of $-90°$ that maps $(6, 0)$ onto $(0, 6)$.

10. $g: x \to 4x$, $h: x \to x^2$. Find the value of $gh(2) - hg(2)$.

11. Give in list form {pairs that may be chosen from W, X, Y, Z}.

12 X denotes reflection in the x-axis, and Y reflection in the y-axis. P is the point (2, 5). Find the coordinates of XY(P).

13 f:x→2x+3, g:x→x². Express gf as a single mapping without brackets

14 Give in list form the most numerous subset of {letters of SECONDARY} which contains no element of {letters of CARES}.

15 A quadrilateral is its own image under a rotation of 180°. What kind of quadrilateral *must* it be? Describe the centre of the rotation.

16 A quadrilateral is its own image under reflection in a diagonal. What kind of quadrilateral *must* it be?

17 A quadrilateral is its own image under reflection in a line which is not a diagonal. What kind of quadrilateral *must* it be? Describe the mirror line of the reflection.

18 The domain set {4, 6, 8, 12, 16, 18} is mapped by the mapping x→prime factor of x. Give the range set. What kind of mapping is this? Is it a function?

19 $\mathscr{E}$={integers between 20 and 30 inclusive},
A={multiples of 5}, B={multiples of 6},
A ⊂ C, and B ⊂ C. Give C in list form if C is to have as few members as possible.

20 R denotes a rotation of 90° about (0, 0) and S a rotation of 90° about (3, 0). Find the coordinates of RS(0, 0).

Exercise 2A – medium-length questions
Part 1

1 f(x) denotes the number of different positive integers, other than 1 and x itself, which are factors of x. For example, since 2, 3, 4, and 6 are factors of 12, then f(12)=4. Write down the values of

    a f(23)   **b** f(24)   **c** f(25)   (CC)

2 In Figure R5 the line BE divides the rectangle ACDF into two equal squares.

    a R is an anticlockwise rotation in the plane of the paper. Under R, triangle ABF is mapped onto triangle CDB. Give the centre and the angle of rotation R.
    b M is a reflection in a certain line. Under M, triangle ABF is mapped onto triangle CBD. Name the line.   (CC)

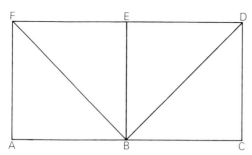

Figure R5

3 $\mathscr{E}=\{4, 5, 6, 7, 8, 9, 10, 11, 12\}$
List the members of the following sets.

    a {multiples of 3}   **c** $\{x: 24-3x=9\}$ **e** $\{z: (z-6)^2=4\}$
    b {factors of 385}   **d** $\{y: 3y>25\}$
                                                                                                                                                               (AEBR)

4 Draw a mapping diagram to illustrate the mapping $x \to$ multiple of x, for the set $\{6, 12, 18, 36\}$.

5 Find the coordinates of the image of the point (6, 1) under a rotation of 90° about (0, 0), followed by a reflection in the line $y=x$.   (16+)

6 $\mathscr{E}=\{$positive integers between 10 and 40 inclusive$\}$. M_2, M_3, M_4, M_5 and M_6 are the sets of multiples of 2, 3, 4, 5 and 6 respectively

    a Give three inclusion relations (i.e. relations involving the symbol $\subset$) between pairs of the above sets.
    b Give in list form the set of integers that are not members of any of the M sets.
    c What is the set of integers that are members of all the M sets? What is the set of integers that are members of four of them?

7 The mappings f and g map x onto $2x+3$ and $4x+a$ respectively. Find $fg(2)$ and $gf(2)$ in terms of a, and find the value of a for which fg and gf are the same mapping.

8 The coordinates of A, B and C are respectively (6, 4), (5, 3) and (7, 3); those of P, Q and R are respectively $(-1, -2)$, $(-1, -1)$ and $(-3, -1)$. Describe completely a single transformation which transforms triangle ABC onto triangle PQR.   (CD)

Part 2

1 A mapping f maps any integer n onto the **remainder** when n is divided by 7. Find the range of f when the domain is

    a {integers}   **b** {perfect squares}   **c** {perfect cubes}

2 ABCDEF is a regular hexagon, the lettering as given running clockwise round the figure, and O is its centre. Name the images of triangle OAB under the following transformations.

    a a rotation of 60° about O   **e** a reflection in OB
    b a rotation of 60° about B   **f** a reflection in CF
    c a rotation of 120° about O   **g** a reflection in the line joining O
    d a rotation of 60° about C   to the mid-point of AF

3 Draw a Venn diagram to represent
$\mathscr{E}$ = {numbers}, R = {rational numbers},
T = {fractions that are equal to terminating decimals}. ('Terminating decimals' means decimals that do not recur.)

In your diagram put small crosses in the appropriate regions and letter them to represent the following numbers:
A to represent $\frac{3}{4}$, B to represent $\frac{2}{3}$, C to represent $\frac{7}{25}$, D to represent $\sqrt{3}$, E to represent $\sqrt{\frac{9}{49}}$, F to represent $\frac{1}{2}\pi$.

4 Describe the mapping represented by Figure R6,

    a if the arrows are in the directions shown
    b if the arrows are in the reverse directions.

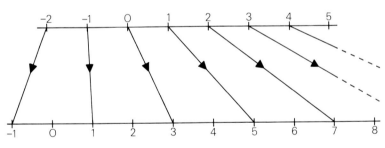

Figure R6

5 ABC is a triangle with AB = 3 cm, BC = 4 cm, CA = 5 cm. The angle ACB may be taken as 37°. A' is the image of A under reflection in BC, and B' is the image of B under reflection in AC. Find all the sides and angles of the quadrilateral AA'CB'.

6 In this question, $\mathscr{E}$ = {animals}, M = {mammals},
F = {animals that can fly}, B = {bats}.
Write in symbols the following sentences.

    a All bats are mammals   **c** Not all mammals are bats
    b All bats can fly

For each of the following statements, say whether the above three facts prove it, or disprove it, or neither.

d All mammals can fly
e Some mammals can fly
f No mammals can fly
g Some animals that can fly are not bats

7 Given that f: x→10−x, find f(3), f(7), ff(3) and ff(7). Express ff' as a single mapping, in as simple a form as possible. g is a mapping such that gg(x)=ff(x). Suggest a mapping that g might be.

8 ABCD is a square, and W, X, Y and Z are the mid-points of its sides, as shown in Figure R7. Name the seven triangles which are congruent to APW, and for each of these triangles describe a transformation that maps APW onto it.

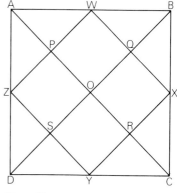

Figure R7

Exercise 2B – longer questions

1 The functions F and f are defined as follows.
F:x→largest prime factor of x (so that, for example, F(6)=3, F(7)=7.
f:x→smallest prime factor of x (so that, for example, f(6)=2, f(7)=7.
Give the values of F(30), f(30), F(31), f(31), F(32), f(32).
Show that if x=F(x), then x=f(x), and name the set of values of x for which these equations hold.
Name three values of x for which F(x)=f(x) but x≠F(x), and make a statement about all values of x for which these relations hold. (*LC*)

2 Using a scale of 1 cm to 1 unit on each axis, draw on graph paper the triangle A, whose vertices are (2, 0), (2, 2), and (5, 2). There should be enough space on the graph paper for x to range from −8 to 8 and y from −2 to 6.

a On your graph paper draw and label
(i) B, the image of A under a reflection in the line y=x
(ii) C, the image of A under a rotation of 90° about the point P(−1, −1)
b Describe fully the single transformation which maps B onto C.
c On your graph draw and label D, the image of A under the combined transformation of a reflection in y=x followed by a rotation of 90° about P.
d Draw the mirror line of the reflection under which D can be mapped onto C. Write down the coordinates of the points where it crosses the axes. (*16+*)

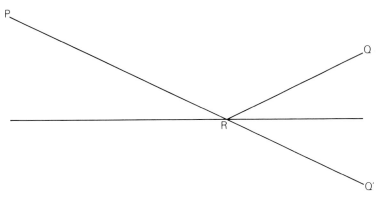

Figure R8

3 In Figure R8, Q' is the image of Q under reflection in the line *l*. The line PQ' meets *l* at R. Show that

a PR and RQ make equal angles with *l*,
b PR+RQ<PS+SQ, where S is any point on *l* other than R.

Draw lines OA and OB such that ∠AOB=40°. Mark the point P so that ∠AOP=15°, ∠BOP=25° and OP=8 cm. Construct P' and P'', the images of P under reflection in OA and OB respectively. Hence construct the triangle PXY such that X and Y lie on OA and OB respectively, and the triangle has the least possible perimeter consistent with these conditions. (*LC*)

4 The functions f and g map x onto $3x-2$ and $2x^2+1$ respectively. Show that fg maps x onto $6x^2+1$, and find the mapping of the function gf. A third function, h, maps x onto $ax+b$, where a and b are positive constants, and is such that fgh maps x onto $6x^2+12x+7$. Find the values of a and b and also that of fgh(-2). (*LC*)

5 The function f maps any integer n onto the remainder when n is divided by 3. Write down two values of n for which f$(n)=1$, and two values for which f$(n)=2$. Show that if f$(n)=1$ and f$(n')=1$, then f$(n+n')=2$.

If n is not a multiple of 3, then either $n=3r+1$ or $n=3r+2$, where r is an integer. By expanding $(3r+1)^2$ and $(3r+2)^2$, show that if n is a perfect square which is not a multiple of 3, then f$(n)=1$.

Use the above results to show that if the sum of two perfect squares is a perfect square, one of them is a multiple of 3.

6 Copy Figure R9.

a Reflect triangle A on the line $y=0$ to give triangle H and draw triangle H on the graph. Label it H.

b Reflect triangle A in the line $y=x$ to give triangle B and draw triangle B on the graph. Label it B.
c Reflect triangle F in the line $y=x$ to give triangle E and draw triangle E on the graph. Label it E.
d Describe single transformations which would map (i) F onto G, (ii) A onto E, (iii) E onto B. *(16+)*

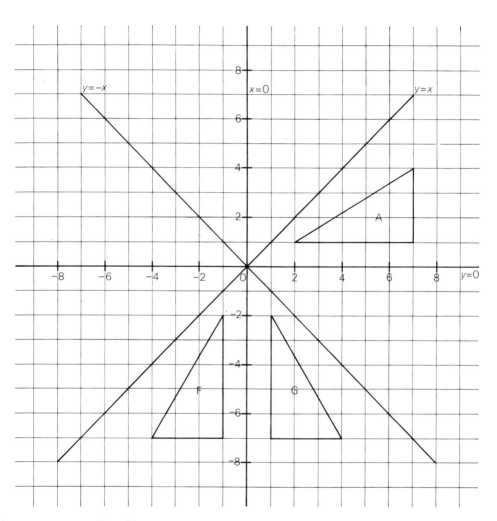

Figure R9

On chapters 6 to 10

Exercise 3S – short questions

1. Give the number 123 456 789 in standard form correct to 4 significant figures.

2. Give the image of the point (3, −4) under the translation whose vector is $\begin{pmatrix} -2 \\ 7 \end{pmatrix}$

3. Find the range of values of x for which $3x - 5 < 7$.

4. A triangle whose sides are 3 cm, 4 cm and 5 cm long is enlarged with a linear scale factor of 5. Find the area of the image triangle.

5. Add the matrices $\begin{pmatrix} 2 & 0 & -3 \\ 5 & 3 & 2 \end{pmatrix}$ and $\begin{pmatrix} -5 & 4 & 7 \\ -3 & 4 & -5 \end{pmatrix}$.

6. Multiply 7×10^4 by 3×10^5, giving the answer in standard form.

7. Find the vector of the translation under which (−4, 6) is the image of (−1, −2).

8. Under a certain enlargement, the points (0, 0) and (1, 0) are mapped onto (0, 1) and (1, 2) respectively. Find the centre and the scale factor of the enlargement.

9. The dimensions of a rectangle are given as 6.1 cm long by 5.1 cm wide, each measurement being correct to 2 significant figures. Find the smallest possible value of its perimeter.

10. AB is a diameter of a circle whose centre is O. Regarding this figure as a network, compile the route matrix for routes between A, B and O.

11. ABCDEF is a regular hexagon whose centre is O. Name three vectors in the figure, all of which are equal to **AB**, and three which are equal to **BA**.

12. Give $\frac{3}{20000}$ as a decimal in standard form.

13. The inequality $\frac{1}{x} > \frac{1}{4}$ is satisfied for values of x in the set $x: a < x < b$. Find the values of a and b.

14 Find x and y if $3\begin{pmatrix} x & 1 \\ 2 & y \end{pmatrix} = \begin{pmatrix} y & 3 \\ 6 & 9 \end{pmatrix}$.

15 Find what distance (in km) is represented by a length of 2.3 cm on a map whose scale is 1:200 000.

16 A wind blowing from a bearing 030 with a speed of 20 m.p.h. is represented by a vector **v**. What wind is represented by a vector $-3\mathbf{v}$?

17 Find $(1.2 \times 10^{-5}) - (8 \times 10^{-6})$ giving the answer in standard form.

18 A firm makes concrete garden ornaments in two sizes. The small-sized ones are 40 cm high and weigh 50 kg each. The larger ones are exactly similar but are 80 cm high. How much does each of the larger ones weigh?

19 A 'Pacific' type steam locomotive had 4 leading wheels, 6 driving wheels and 2 trailing wheels. An 'Atlantic' type locomotive was the same except that it had only 4 driving wheels. A 'Consolidation' type had two leading and 8 driving wheels, with no trailing wheels. Compile a 3×3 matrix to summarise this information.

20 Find the set of possible values of x, if x is an integer and $x \leqslant 5 < 2x$.

Exercise 3A – medium-length questions

Part 1

1 **a** The number 34 500 can be written in the standard form $K \times 10^4$. Find K.
b The number 0.000 456 can be written in the standard form 4.56×10^n. Find n.
c Express 0.0789 in the standard form $A \times 10^n$ where n is an integer and $1 \leqslant A < 10$.
d Evaluate $(4 \times 10^3) + (5 \times 10^2)$. (*AEB*, 1978)

2 If $\begin{pmatrix} 1 & 2 \\ 3 & y \end{pmatrix} + \begin{pmatrix} 5 & 7 \\ 9 & 4 \end{pmatrix} = \begin{pmatrix} 6 & 9 \\ x & 7 \end{pmatrix}$, calculate
a x **b** y (*AEB*)

3 A model of a lorry is made on a scale of 1 to 10.

a The windscreen of the model has an area of 100 cm². Calculate the area, in square centimetres, of the windscreen of the lorry.
b The fuel tank of the lorry, when full, holds 100 litres. Calculate the capacity, in cubic centimetres, of the fuel tank on the model. (*AEB*, 1976)

4   On graph paper draw axes and mark the point B such that $\overrightarrow{OB} = \begin{pmatrix} 4 \\ 2 \end{pmatrix}$ where O is (0, 0). Write $\overrightarrow{BC}$ as a column vector, where C is the point (6, 7).

Draw CD such that $\overrightarrow{CD} = \begin{pmatrix} 4 \\ -2 \end{pmatrix}$.

Draw OE such that $\overrightarrow{OE} = \begin{pmatrix} 0 \\ 4 \end{pmatrix}$.

Join EB and write $\overrightarrow{EB}$ in vector form.
State two relations between the lines EB and CD.   (16+)

5   Given that $\mathscr{E}$ = {natural numbers excluding zero}, find the solution sets for each of the following.

   a {x: 2x + 4 = 10}   c {x: 3 ⩽ x + 1 < 6}
   b {x: x − 1 < 2}   d {x: $x^2 - 9 \leq 0$}   (16+)

6   Find the length of the hypotenuse of a right-angled triangle, given that the lengths of the other two sides are 20 cm and 21 cm. (The length of the hypotenuse is an exact number of centimetres.)

    A similar right-angled triangle has a hypotenuse which is 2.03 cm long. Calculate the lengths of the other two sides.   (LC)

7   The coordinates of P, Q and R are respectively (1, 2), (4, 6) and (12, 0). Write as column vectors **PQ**, **QR** and **RP**. Find the lengths of these vectors and hence, or otherwise, prove that PQR is a right-angled triangle.

8   Given that $a = 2 \times 10^{-5}$, $b = 4 \times 10^7$ and $c = 8 \times 10^6$,

   a find the value of $\frac{ac}{b}$,
   b solve the equation $ax + b = c$,

   giving both answers in standard form.

Part 2

1   Compile a 4 × 4 matrix to represent the relation 'is a factor of' between the set {3, 6, 12, 24}.

2   $\mathscr{E}$ = {positive integers}
    A = {x: 5x + 3 < 2x + 17}
    B = {x: 10 − x > 5 + x}
    Show that B ⊂ A, and write down the numbers that are members of A but not of B.

REVISION EXERCISES ON CHAPTERS 6 TO 10   181

3 A model M is a scale model of a solid S. The scale factor for any length from M to the corresponding length of S is 2.5×10^4. Calculate, in standard form,

a the scale factor for volume from M to S,
b the scale factor for length from S to M. (*LC*)

4 The coordinates of the points A, B and C are (1, −2), (1, −1) and (3, −1) respectively. A translation maps A onto P, whose coordinates are (1, 4).

a Write down the vector of the translation, and the coordinates of Q and R, the images of B and C under it.

b ABC can be mapped onto PQR by two successive reflections. If the mirror line for the first of these reflections is $y=1$, find the equation of the mirror line for the second.

c Find the vector of the translation which is equivalent to the same two reflections applied in the reverse order.

5 One-third of an even number is less than 8, and one-quarter of the same number is more than 5. Find the number.

6 Draw the network corresponding to the following route matrix.

$$\begin{array}{c} \\ A \\ B \\ C \\ D \end{array} \begin{pmatrix} A & B & C & D \\ 0 & 1 & 0 & 0 \\ 1 & 0 & 1 & 1 \\ 0 & 1 & 0 & 2 \\ 0 & 1 & 2 & 0 \end{pmatrix}$$

This network represents the system of roads connecting four villages. A new road is made connecting D with A and A with B. Compile the new route matrix.

7 ABCD is a rectangle. X and Y are the mid-points of BC and CD respectively, W is a point on AB such that AW:WB = 2:1, and Z is a point on AD such that AZ:ZD = 2:1.

Prove that triangles AWZ and CYX are similar, and that WZ is parallel to XY.

WY crosses XZ at O. Find the ratio WO:OY and the ratio of the areas of triangles WOZ and XOY.

8 Giving all the answers in standard form, find

a the number of millimetres in 6370 km (the radius of the earth)
b the number of microseconds in an hour (a microsecond is a millionth of a second)
c an inch (2.54 cm) expressed as a decimal of a kilometre,
d a square inch expressed as a decimal of a square metre.

Exercise 3B – longer questions

1 For any positive integer n, $T(n)$ is defined as the smallest multiple of 3 which is larger than or equal to n, e.g. $T(5)=6$, $T(6)=6$.

  a Write down the value of $T(9)$ and that of $T(10)$.
  b Give the solution set of the equation $T(n)=12$.
  c State whether each of the following equations is satisfied by all values of n, by some values of n, or by no values of n. Give the solution set of each equation which is satisfied by some values of n.
  (i) $T(n+1)=T(n)+1$
  (ii) $T(n+3)=T(n)+3$
  (iii) $T(2n)=2T(n)$ (LC)

2 In Figure R10, the triangle OAB is right-angled at A. The triangle OPQ is an enlargement of triangle OAB with centre O and scale factor k. The line OCR is the image of OBQ under reflection in the line OP. The line CQ crosses OP at X. Show that triangle XPQ is an enlargement of triangle XAC and state the scale factor in terms of k. Hence show that

$$\frac{CX}{XQ}=\frac{OC}{OQ}$$

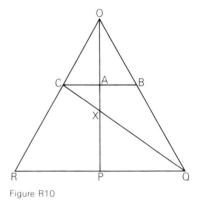

Figure R10

If triangle OAB is taken to have unit area, calculate, in terms of k, the areas of triangles OPQ, OQR and OCQ. (LC)

3 The mass of an atom of hydrogen is approximately 1.66×10^{-24} g, and that of an atom of oxygen is approximately 2.66×10^{-23} g.

  a Find, giving the answer in standard form to three significant figures, the mass of a molecule of water, which consists of two atoms of hydrogen and one of oxygen.
  b The given masses are correct to three significant figures. Find the maximum possible error in your answer to **a**, and show that this answer is not necessarily *correct* to three significant figures. For parts **c** and **d**, use your answer to **a**, approximating it to *two* significant figures.
  c Find, giving your answer in standard form, the approximate number of molecules in 1 g of water.
  d Find, to the nearest whole number, the percentage by mass of oxygen in water. (LC)

4 a On squared paper, with origin O, plot, label and join the points A(-3, 4), B(-3, -4) and C(4, -3). Use a scale of 2 cm to 1 unit on

each axis.
b If **OT** = **OA** + **OC**, find **OT** (as a column vector) and mark T on your diagram.
c If **OH** = **OB** + **OT**, find **OH** and mark H on your diagram.
d If **OG** = $\frac{1}{3}$(**OA** + **OB** + **OC**), find **OG** and mark G on your diagram.
e State the relation between the points O, G and H. *(SMP)*

5 The relation between a Fahrenheit temperature $F°$ and the corresponding Celsius temperature $C°$ is

$$F = \frac{9C}{5} + 32$$

Find the value of F when $C = 15$, and the value of C when $F = 60$.

A rough rule, suitable for rapid mental calculations, is 'To find the Fahrenheit temperature, double the Celsius temperature and add 30'. Write down the relation between F and C corresponding to this rough rule, and find what it gives for the Fahrenheit equivalent of 15°C.

By forming and solving an equation, find the Celsius temperature for which the rough rule agrees with the correct formula. Find also the correct range of Celsius temperatures for which the rough rule gives a result in error by less than 3°F. *(LC)*

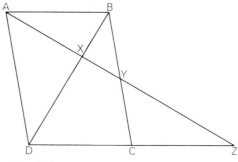

Figure R11

6 In Figure R11, ABCD is a parallelogram, and X is the point on BD such that DX = 3XB. The line AX produced meets BC at Y and DC produced at Z.

a Prove that triangle AXB is similar to triangle ZXD. (Candidates may use any appropriate method. If transformations are used they must be precisely described.)
b Name the triangle similar to triangle BXY.
c Calculate the numerical values of the ratios

(i) $\dfrac{AB}{DZ}$, (ii) $\dfrac{\triangle ABX}{\triangle ZDX}$, (iii) $\dfrac{AB}{CZ}$, (iv) $\dfrac{\triangle ABX}{\triangle ZCY}$ *(CD)*